Battle Fatigue

Understanding PTSD and Finding a Cure

Col. Paul D. Walker (Ret)

iUniverse, Inc.
New York Bloomington

Battle Fatigue
Understanding PTSD and Finding a Cure

Copyright © 2008 Col. Paul D. Walker (Ret)
All rights reserved. No part of this book may be used or reproduced by any means, graphic, electronic, or mechanical, including photocopying, recording, taping or by any information storage retrieval system without the written permission of the publisher except in the case of brief quotations embodied in critical articles and reviews.

The views expressed in this work are solely those of the author and do not necessarily reflect the views of the publisher, and the publisher hereby disclaims any responsibility for them.

iUniverse books may be ordered through booksellers or by contacting:
iUniverse
1663 Liberty Drive
Bloomington, IN 47403
www.iuniverse.com
1-800-Authors (1-800-288-4677)

Because of the dynamic nature of the Internet, any Web addresses or links contained in this book may have changed since publication and may no longer be valid. The views expressed in this work are solely those of the author and do not necessarily reflect the views of the publisher, and the publisher hereby disclaims any responsibility for them.

ISBN: 978-0-595-52996-4 (pbk)
ISBN: 978-0-595-51901-9 (hc)
ISBN: 978-0-595-63050-9 (ebk)

Printed in the United States of America

iUniverse rev. date: 12/18/08

Disclaimer

The book *Battle Fatigue* is not intended as a substitute for professional medical advice; its purpose is to inform and educate the reader.

Contents

Disclaimer v

Acknowledgments ix

Preface xi

Introduction xiii

Chapter One 1
The Face of Battle Fatigue

Chapter Two 20
The Hidden Casualties Among Us: A Short History

Chapter Three 41
The Story of George Barr

Chapter Four 64
Diagnosis and Treatment

Chapter Five 84
Stories from the Front Line

Chapter Six 104
Summary and Recommendations

Appendix A 113
Resource List

Appendix B 117
Stars and Stripes Articles

Appendix C 147
Symptoms of Traumatic Stress/Battle Fatigue

Bibliography 157

Acknowledgments

A book like *Battle Fatigue* rarely gets put together through the efforts of one person alone, and I would be remiss if I failed to express my deepest gratitude to those key individuals who provided their generous assistance to make it happen. First, to my wife, Virgilia, who offered much advice on how to organize and design the various chapters for greater clarity, I thank you. Then, for their professional and detailed editing of the book, to include suggestions for expanding and improving different sections, I'm particularly grateful to Jerry McClure, Commander, United States Navy (retired) and to Michael "Mik" Mikulan, Commander, United States Public Health Service (retired) both are aviators. To these three fine individuals, I extend my sincerest and warmest gratitude.

Preface

This book is dedicated to all who have served our great nation, past, present, and future. I salute you. The book is for you, your family, friends, neighbors, doctors, nurses, or anyone you want to involve in this journey to greater understanding and well-being.

As one who has spent thirty-two years in the military at various levels of command, I've experienced firsthand and have been in the presence of those who have suffered from this condition, which was often not given a name. At the time, neither active duty doctors nor the Veterans Administration had an effective treatment for this disorder and, usually, the individual was discharged back into the civilian community to find his own cure. Only during the last few years have military doctors begun to recognize "Battle Fatigue" and Post-Traumatic Stress Disorder (PTSD) as legitimate injuries and to actively treat them.

My interest in writing this book has been to educate service members, the general public, and particularly military leaders about the disabling effects of a mental condition commonly known as Battle Fatigue. It is my hope that, through a greater understanding of this condition, veterans may find the treatment they need, and military leaders will be better able to plan for and avoid Battle Fatigue casualties in all future combat operations.

Those unfamiliar with Battle Fatigue will often confuse it with cowardice or "cowardice in the face of the enemy." This is certainly not the case. *The New World Dictionary* defines *coward* as "a person who lacks courage, especially one who is shamefully unable to control his fear and so shrinks from danger or trouble." With Battle Fatigue, the reverse is true: the individuals affected by this condition have been exposed to intense combat for a prolonged period of time, and virtually all would willingly return to combat if ordered to do so.

The exact cause of this condition, which can produce lifelong disabilities, is little understood. However, recent case histories have shown that it affects not just the veteran but also his entire family and all those who come in contact with him.

This book is designed to provide a better understanding of the causes and effects of this serious condition and create a greater appreciation for the psychological damage and health care costs to the nation that all wars bring. Part of its message is that effective treatment does exist for sufferers of Battle Fatigue and that veterans and their families should make every effort to find these solutions. Finally, it is a challenge to all of us to help change those things in military institutions and culture that needlessly create or worsen these injuries.

Additionally, in the aftermath of recent terrorist attacks around the world and as U.S. forces remain heavily engaged in the Middle East, it would be helpful to remind the American people and our senior military commanders of the importance of safeguarding our service members from all forms of injury, including the very subtle effects of Battle Fatigue.

Introduction

The cost of America's wars in the Middle East is not always measured in dollars and cents but often in the number of broken lives they produce. This is a story about some of those broken lives—the hundreds of thousands of Battle Fatigue veterans who are part of our society today and are sometimes referred to as "the silent casualties among us." It is a triumph of modern medicine that a much higher percentage of these wounded troops are coming home from the wars in the Middle East. But many of these veterans return hobbled by prolonged physical and mental injuries, mainly caused from powerful improvised explosive devices and the much more sophisticated roadside bombs made in Iran. This "no front lines" type of war, with its sudden terror, is what increases the anxiety and seriousness of these psychological injuries. The National Center for PTSD estimates that as high as one in three of our servicemen and servicewomen are returning with some level of Post-Traumatic Stress Disorder (PTSD). As of August 2008, that number could be over 450,000.

Every day, hundreds of U.S. service personnel complete their tours of duty and return to America from distant battlefields with strange-sounding names like Kandahar, Kabul, and Baghdad. Most will quickly readjust to the routine of family, home, and garrison duty. However, a growing percentage will not be able to put their fears or nightmarish experiences behind them and move on. These unfortunate souls will be tormented for years by the demons that follow them. They will then join the growing ranks of the silent casualties among us. Although these men and women suffer from a condition first documented over 3,000 years ago, it is still little understood by the general population and especially by those in the military who are responsible for preventing it.

Prior to World War I, the U.S. Army considered the symptoms of Battle Fatigue to be cowardice behavior or an attempt by the individual to avoid the dangers of combat. Little thought was given to the possibility that it could be a real medical condition, and many of these unfortunate servicemen received very harsh treatment from their chain of command; some even faced the firing squad for their symptoms. As one can imagine, this reaction by military leaders led to few Battle Fatigue casualties showing up at field hospitals.

Today, military doctors and health care workers are very much aware of the causes, symptoms, and severe damage this condition can produce in a military person's life and the lives of those around them. On the other hand, military leaders on the operational side still act as if they are clueless regarding this condition and provide little training to combat leaders on the subject, nor do they consult medical personnel as they plan and conduct combat operations. If they had any understanding at all, they would never arbitrarily extend large numbers of soldiers from twelve to fifteen months or send injured troops back for multiple tours. Only as an afterthought are medical personnel brought in to treat the Battle Fatigue casualties that intense and prolonged combat produces.

In recent memory, only one senior military leader has addressed this problem and, even then, inadvertently. General Colin Powell, former chairman of the Joint Chiefs of Staff, with his "Powell Doctrine" required overwhelming force or in his words, "a sledge hammer to kill a gnat" in every military operation to insure success and reduce our casualties. Without intending to, this policy also reduced Battle Fatigue casualties. But as Powell moved on, it was quickly forgotten, and as in the case of Iraq, the policy was shifted back to requiring the minimum force necessary to accomplish the mission.

It has always been a challenging task to take young men and women directly off the streets of the nation's towns and cities and prepare them to fight on a modern battlefield. Accomplishing this requires that a long list of subjects be taught in a limited amount of time. As a result, many topics such as Battle Fatigue are never covered, despite the fact that, in some units with numerous redeployments, as high as 100 percent are returning with some degree of PTSD or mental trauma. The solution seems apparent: to persuade senior military leaders to include this important subject in all military schools and blocks of instruction dealing with combat and to lift the stigma from those seeking treatment. Only then will the mental health and well-being of our service members be considered when planning future military operations.

Battle Fatigue is also known by other names, such as "shell shock," "battle stress," post-traumatic stress disorder," and "psychologically wounded." These little-known or little-understood conditions, which result from a prolonged exposure to severe death and destruction, have been observed and recorded since the days of ancient Greece. The term most Americans are familiar with, "post-traumatic stress disorder," has been used recently to describe many other groups and conditions such as abused children, battered spouses, rape victims, or those involved in serious accidents—anything that has left an emotional scar on a victim. The term this book will focus on is Battle Fatigue, a condition that is directly related to military service and is broader in its definition than PTSD. The discussion of this very sensitive issue is narrated from the standpoint of a combat veteran who has witnessed firsthand, the traumatic conditions being described, and it focuses on a narrow category of psychological injuries that result from intense military combat.

The historical narrative is used throughout this book to reinforce the fact that PTSD is not something new; it has been around since mankind first engaged in mortal combat. Therefore, psychologically injured soldiers of the twenty-first century must understand that they are just the latest casualties of this ancient injury.

In a more focused effort to educate, the book examines the last three major wars, with particular attention to Afghanistan and Iraq,

Col. Paul D. Walker (Ret)

for examples and causes of Battle Fatigue. Then, citing my own experience and through personal interviews with veterans and health care professionals, it examines the latest treatments available—many that actually work. Then to offer hope, the book takes a look at how veterans currently suffering from Battle Fatigue are getting their lives back together.

CHAPTER ONE

The Face of Battle Fatigue

Soon after the president's decision to invade Iraq, former Secretary of Defense Donald Rumsfeld and his region commander, Gen. Tommy Franks, put together an invasion force that was high in technology but low in manpower. This meant that, once the battle commenced, ground forces would be stretched to the maximum and expected to handle several missions at the same time, placing a heavy burden on those chosen to lead the fight.

The following is a brief narrative of the opening battle of the Iraq War. It is designed to show how, even on the modern battlefield, the subtle effects of Battle Fatigue can surface during intense and prolonged combat.

Following a massive bombardment, the famed 3rd Infantry Division blasted across the Kuwaiti border and into Iraq. The unit "spearheading" this assault was the 3rd Squadron of the 7th Cavalry Regiment, a unit of approximately one thousand men, which, for its size, had been given a huge mission. In the lead, the highly mobile 3/7 Cavalry was to smash through the sand barriers of the Kuwaiti border and drive north toward Baghdad, seizing two bridges in the town of Samawah while protecting the right flank of the division as it moved. Once the division had passed over the bridges, the 3/7 Cavalry would serve as a decoy to confuse the enemy by attacking north on a different highway than the main force. Then, at a given point, they would engage a major Iraqi unit, the Medina Division, to keep it from interfering with the movement of the main force.

This was a large mission that was normally assigned to a unit three times its size, but the 3/7 was promised plenty of help in the form of allied warplanes, helicopters, and lots of artillery. The unit was also told that there was a very good chance that the enemy would offer little resistance, and they might even be greeted with flowers and little American flags in the towns and villages they liberated.

This, of course, did not happen. From its initial entry into the hostile country, the unit had to endure rain and high winds that reduced visibility and turned the dirt roads into tons of thick mud, which added to the stress of the situation. Then, as the unit approached its objective at Samawah, it was attacked by an enemy force of uniformed regulars and irregulars wearing civilian clothes, both groups firing AK-47 rifles, antitank guns, and mortars. The battle for the bridges raged on for two days and involved fierce hand-to-hand fighting, resulting in hundreds of Iraqi soldiers killed or wounded and dozens of American casualties, together with several armored vehicles destroyed or damaged. Fought virtually house-to-house, the round-the-clock battle was particularly tense. The enemy, dressed in "street" clothes, had used women and children as shields, while driving reinforcements around the battlefield in trucks clearly marked as ambulances.

The 3/7 Cavalry had been in constant contact with the enemy for over two days when help finally did arrive, but rather than standing down or allowing the unit time to rest and refit, it was given a new mission to move west and occupy a blocking position at a supposedly safe highway intersection. Starting their third day without sleep, the entire unit began to experience the subtle effects of Battle Fatigue, as exhaustion clouded the heads of those planning the next phase of the battle. In receiving his new instructions from higher headquarters, the squadron commander misunderstood map coordinates, and the unit dashed off in the wrong direction. Within hours, this small error would lead to dire consequences for the unit.

As the squadron moved out, drivers and crew members were stretched to the breaking point, some dozing at their battle stations, and accidents began to happen when vehicles collided on mud slick roads, in some cases leading to serious injuries.

The tired troopers of the 3/7 Cavalry, now traveling on the wrong road, approached the town of Faysailiyah, where they ran headlong into a well-coordinated ambush and immediately began to take heavy casualties. Fatigue and the "fog of war" pulled at the commander as he struggled to remove his unit. Adding to his difficulties was the time of day; it was late evening, and dark shadows were already beginning to form as he tried desperately to contact higher headquarters for assistance. The air was heavy with machine-gun fire and antitank rounds as casualties quickly began to mount, with several vehicles blown up or set on fire at the front of the column. Still unable to make radio contact with higher headquarters, the commander was on his own, deep in enemy territory, with few options, so he ordered his rear platoon to circle around and find a way out of the ambush. Not operating at the top of his game, the platoon leader quickly executed the order and soon radioed that he had found a way around the ambush site but cautioned that the squadron would have to cross a narrow, frail-looking bridge.

With the wounded loaded aboard vehicles that could still operate, the squadron now began to reverse course to follow the new route. Then suddenly a frantic call came from the lead platoon leader informing the commander that the narrow bridge had collapsed, leaving five of his armored vehicles isolated on the far side.

With time now running out, the squadron commander ordered the five stranded vehicles on the far side of the river to do their best to find a way out and rejoin the main body. The rest of the squadron was ordered to turn around in place, return to the main road and simply charge through the ambush site with all guns blazing and just hope for the best.

Catching the enemy by surprise, the unit was able to blast through the old ambush site. They then spent the remainder of the night coiled on the highway just north of the small town. At first light, the squadron commander's radio sputtered to life as an angry assistant division commander's voice boomed through loud and clear, demanding to know where the unit was and why they hadn't completed their assigned mission, unaware that the squadron had spent the night on the wrong road in a vicious gun battle. Soldiers of the squadron desperately needed rest, but the general explained that events were going badly for a nearby unit, and he needed their big guns to pull them out. Quickly explaining the overall situation, the general then outlined a new mission for the battered unit that required them to move out immediately with everything that was operational and try to rescue the surrounded unit.

This new mission required the squadron to secure objective Floyd, which included seizing another bridge and protecting the approaches to the city of Najaf, drawing the enemy's attention and taking the pressure off the embattled unit. The unexpected assignment would involve two more days of intense combat for the war-weary soldiers of the 3/7 Cavalry. With this last mission accomplished, the exhausted 3/7 was finally given an opportunity to rest and refit.

The sequence of events that I've outlined above is not at all unusual for units in combat. As all military leaders know, the mission comes first, and only then do you look after the welfare of your troops. But because the United States went into Iraq with limited forces, all of the units committed to combat, not just the 3/7, were required to carry an extra-heavy burden. Part of that burden for the valiant commander of the 3/7 Cavalry and his courageous men would be exposing them all to the very likely possibility of becoming Battle Fatigue casualties.

Due to its various effects on the mind and body, Battle Fatigue is not easily defined, but the following is the best description that I've found that encompasses all aspects of the injury: Battle Fatigue is caused primarily by an individual being involved in a traumatic event or witnessing one. This individual could also be subjected to the severe state of "fight or flight" that one experiences when confronted by, for example, an artillery barrage during a prolonged period of time or traveling over roads mined with Improvised Explosive Devices (IEDs). These are potentially life-threatening events, over which we have no control and to which we are unable to respond effectively no matter how hard we try. A lack of sleep or of rest increases the effects of this condition, and witnessing the events again can produce the same results.

Traumatic experiences that the mind cannot process are what cause many of the casualties that later show up at the field hospitals or on the home front as Battle Fatigue. In diagnosing this condition, there are specific symptoms that health care providers look for. To establish a baseline for discussing these symptoms, I've listed a summary below of the four criteria that have been agreed upon by the American Psychiatric Association as a diagnosis for Battle Fatigue, often referred to as post-traumatic stress disorder.

1. A sense of foreshortened future and a need to be armed for self-protection

2. A constant search for danger and the adrenalin rush of combat

3. An inability to sleep/fragmented sleep, with traumatic dreams that relive episodes of combat, hyper-vigilance, and exaggerated startle reflexes

4. Social withdrawal, a display of hostility, isolation, an inability to express affection, or thoughts of suicide

With most combat veterans, there is a period lasting normally a few weeks to a few months following intense combat, when the individual experiences a variety of the symptoms listed above, plus disbelief, numbness, fatigue, fear, and finally guilt for having survived while so many others perished. Some may have trouble sleeping, while others may have recurrent memories of the event. All of these post-combat reactions are normal, and, within a few weeks, most are able to put these events behind them and move on with their lives. However, there is currently a growing percentage, 20–25 percent of this population, that has difficulty returning to normal duty; instead, they continue to experience these symptoms over a prolonged period of time. With these soldiers, the events experienced or witnessed were so intensely traumatic that their minds and bodies were unable to move beyond them and, in some cases, they continue to experience these same traumatic events over and over in their dreams or subconscious thoughts for the remainder of their lives.

After serving two, three, or even four tours of duty in the present war in Iraq or Afghanistan, many servicemen and women have returned with anxieties that a close psychological examination would reveal as being directly caused by the fact that they actually miss the presence of danger and the thrill of a "close call."

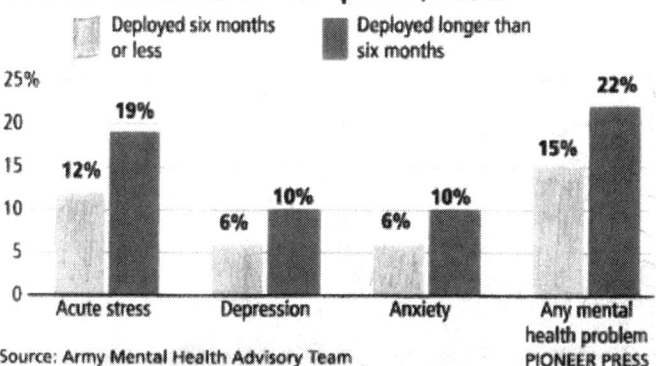

In the past, this particular condition has not been well diagnosed or well understood, and medical personnel as well as commanders viewed the individual who was unable to settle down and quickly adjust to a normal duty routine as totally unfit for further duty. The condition was thought to be permanent, and the soldier was looked upon as unreliable and unpredictable. The next step would be action by his chain of command to separate the individual and return him to civilian status as soon as possible with a less than honorable discharge

The example we are most familiar with is the soldier who, after his return from intense combat, is quiet, withdrawn, and just wants to be left alone. This condition is attributed to the individual having been so frightened by his combat experience that he doesn't want to repeat it. He also feels that his luck has "run out," causing him to be seized with a strong anxiety that in the next battle he will be killed.

Despite the neutral statements above, a misunderstanding or misdiagnosis of the condition is not a thing of the past, as a recent article in *USA Today* shows: "Marines who performed well in combat

(Iraq) can be lauded for it. But if they developed PTSD (or Battle Fatigue) they can be punished for stress-related misconduct, kicked out of the military, and denied treatment for their illness." An ongoing investigation has revealed that over one thousand Marines may have been "kicked out" for demonstrating symptoms of Battle Fatigue.

As large as some of these numbers are, military leaders should be aware that statistics clearly show that, for most service members, Battle Fatigue is a temporary condition, and most who suffer from it require only a brief period of time before being able to return to normal duty. Early identification seems to be the key to a successful recovery, and most who are diagnosed with these symptoms can be placed in a program of treatment that will allow them to quickly return to duty. The small remainder who can't recover from Battle Fatigue after this treatment are normally discharged as fully functioning members of society. However, in a very small number of cases, continued involvement by a Veteran's Administration physician or counselor is necessary over an extended period of time.

With the large-scale involvement in Iraq of our reserve components, sometimes referred to as citizen soldiers but officially known as the National Guard and Reserves, conditions are even more likely to produce Battle Fatigue. This is, in part, because these civilian soldiers are unexpectedly "called up" (no matter how much training or warning they receive, it's always a surprise) and taken from their regular occupations, with the complicated job and family arrangements this entails. Then, leaving a wife and family on their own for twelve to sixteen months in a small town or city, away from the usual support groups and facilities normally available for active duty families, further complicates the condition. Experience has shown that the reserve component servicemen and servicewomen have a more difficult time than their active duty counterparts, in balancing civilian occupations and family responsibilities before leaving on long deployments. Add to this, double and triple tours to combat areas, and the mounting stress increases their chances of becoming a Battle Fatigue casualty. Additionally, as this group returns to civilian life, the symptoms take longer to emerge and are more difficult to detect.

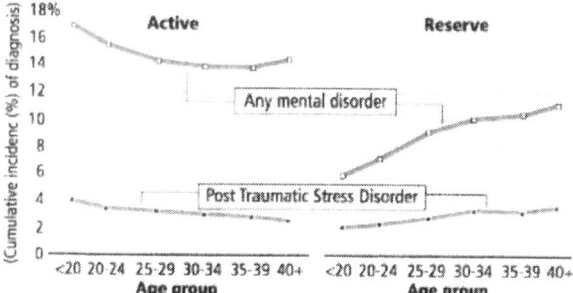

Source: Department of Defense Medical Surveillance Monthly Report, July 2007
PIONEER PRESS

With the large number of veterans in our society today, who have been affected by Battle Fatigue and with the subject having been so widely written about, it's difficult to understand why there are still so many, particularly senior, leaders in our armed forces who have little or no knowledge of this condition. For these individuals, I often use the following example from my own military background to help explain.

Many years ago, as a newly commissioned second lieutenant, I was sent to Fort Knox, Kentucky, to learn about tanks. One of our blocks of instruction covered tank radios and mobile communications. In the first session, the students were introduced to the platoon leader's radio, a large multi-knobbed, Korean War vintage AN/GRC-24. As we began to familiarize ourselves with the device, many of the students were intrigued by a protected switch on the upper right hand corner of the radio face. This switch was painted red and labeled "Combat Override."

It was explained to us that, when the radio was transmitting, a tremendous amount of heat was generated and, at a certain temperature, in order to prevent damage, it would automatically shut itself off. Addressing the combat override switch, the instructor's voice became very serious as he said, "Only in the gravest, most desperate situations, would you use the combat override switch to continue transmitting." He added, "With the switch on, you can continue transmitting and accomplish your mission, but components of the radio will be permanently damaged, and in the process, you may destroy the entire radio."

The results are the same when a commander is forced to throw the "combat override switch." He is sometimes compelled to keep his men in heavy combat for too long or to subject them to more severe conditions than they were trained for, are prepared for, or are capable of withstanding. Although the mission may be accomplished, the results are the same as with the radio: permanent injury and psychological damage to the soldiers.

As previously stated, those who have chosen the military as a career are fully aware that there are times when the mission assumes a greater importance than the lives and well-being of their men and equipment. However, these occasions are thankfully rare, and by making military leaders of all ranks aware of the causes and symptom of Battle Fatigue, they will be better able to recognize and, where possible, avoid or lessen the conditions that lead to psychological injuries.

Commanders can be trained to lessen the causes of this condition by, among other things, deploying an overwhelming force, assigning appropriate missions to units, rotating men off the "line" on a more reasonable basis, and assigning personnel to positions and tasks that they are physically and emotionally qualified to perform. But this is not always possible. Since the end of the "cold war," the Defense Department has sought to reduce the size of the armed forces and, in the case of the army, has virtually cut the force in half. Then along comes the terrorist attacks of 9/11, which led to the missions to invade and conquer Afghanistan and Iraq. This reduced force was unable to accomplish its mission without the additional strength of the guard and reserve—just the sort of circumstance that forces commanders, because of limited manpower to keep troops in highly stressful situations too long and then, within a short period, with little time for military personnel to "decompress," bring them back for multiple tours, making soldiers ripe for Battle Fatigue.

History's most famous examples of a failure to recognize Battle Fatigue as a legitimate illness or injury occurred during World War II and involved one of America's icons of aggressive warfare, Gen. George S. Patton, Jr.

Col. Paul D. Walker (Ret)

The following account of Gen. Patton's notorious encounter with an unfortunate soldier illustrates the sort of prejudice and misunderstanding that surrounds Battle Fatigue. I've devoted considerable space to this incident, because military men for generations have, and still do, pattern themselves after the famous general. This imitation includes Patton's disdain for anyone's inability to withstand the withering onslaught of constant and intense combat.

"In July 1942, Great Britain and America decided that their first joint offensive of the war would be an invasion of French North Africa. Major General Dwight D. Eisenhower, the American commander of the European Theatre of Operations, was given the authority to choose his own assault commanders. The first commander he picked was his longtime friend, whose reputation for aggressiveness was well known—George Patton."

"Eisenhower gave his old acquaintance the potentially toughest assignment, that of hitting the beach at Casablanca. Then, in March 1943, following the battle of the Kasserine Pass, Patton was brought to Tunisia to take command of the U.S. Army's II corps, which had been badly battered. His instructions were to restore morale and raise the image of American troops in British eyes by winning a victory or two. With his usual skill and boldness, he quickly accomplished these tasks."

Patton had always been a martinet when it came to morale. He himself indulged in gaudy uniforms but insisted that his enlisted men dress meticulously according to regulation, even in the front lines. He worked them hard, subjecting them to twice as many drills, and training exercised as most generals. He used these techniques with the II Corps, and they worked. In addition, he made his men shave regularly and stand straight, and in the next battle, he scored a tactical victory over the great German tank commander, Erwin Rommel. A grateful Eisenhower then gave Patton the most coveted combat position in the army—command of the invasion of Sicily.

Patton did well. His Seventh Army sent the German and Italian opposition reeling across Sicily past Palermo. When he turned his army east for the drive to Messina, across from the Italian "toe," the Germans were waiting. Progress was exasperatingly slow. The narrow roads, winding through the mountains, gave the Germans every advantage. Patton was almost beside himself.

On August 3, while he was in this mood, he tried to make himself feel better in a way that had often worked well before: he visited an evacuation hospital near the front and talked to brave soldiers who had recently been wounded in action. This time, it backfired. The general had gone around the hospital tent and chatted with a number of bandaged men, asking them how they got wounded, where they were from, and so on. Then he came to Private C. H. Kuhl, a young infantryman from Mishawka, Indiana. Kuhl was sitting on a "C" ration box and had no visible signs of a wound. To Patton's first question, the soldier said simply, "I guess I can't take it." As Patton admitted later, he "flew off the handle." In his opinion, most cases of "shell shock" or Battle Fatigue were just plain cowardice, and he proceeded to say so to Kuhl in a high, excited voice and with an appropriate selection from his rich storehouse of profanity. Then he slapped Kuhl across the face with his gloves and turned to the medical officer in charge, shouting, "Don't admit this son of a bitch. I don't want yellow-bellied bastards like this hiding their lousy cowardice around here, stinking up this place of honor!" Patton then stalked out. Kuhl, who had been admitted to the hospital on a diagnosis of psychoneurotic anxiety, was found, upon further examination, to have chronic diarrhea, malaria, and a temperature of 102.2° F.

Patton felt that he had done the right thing, and he dictated a brief account of the episode for inclusion in his diary, adding the following in his own hand: "One sometimes slaps a baby to bring it to." He then issued a memorandum to the officers of his command, directing that any soldiers pretending to be "nervously incapable of combat" should not be sent to a hospital, but, if they refused to fight, should be "tried by court-martial for cowardice in the face of the enemy" (Ambrose 1997).

About a week later, Patton repeated the incident. This time, he hit the soldier twice, then drew one of his pearl-handled pistols and threatened to shoot the soldier on the spot.

It was impossible to keep the incidents quiet, and soon every newspaper in America had the story. The reaction was so strong that Eisenhower was forced to remove Patton from command. (The Patton story was inspired by *Americans at War*, Ambrose, 2004.)

The damage from these incidents extended far beyond the two men involved. As word of the incidents spread throughout U.S. forces, thousands of men who might have sought treatment for Battle Fatigue hesitated to come forward, for fear of being branded a coward or a malingerer or possibly facing a court-martial.

As mentioned earlier, Gen. Patton is a hero to many and a role model to countless others. Even today, great numbers of officers and sergeants pattern their styles of leadership around the image he created. Unfortunately, this image is totally unsympathetic and lacking in all understanding for the condition of Battle Fatigue.

Another combat injury that Gen. Patton would not be sympathetic toward is Traumatic Brain Injury (TBI). This condition also has no outward signs of injury, but the symptoms are, in many cases, similar to those of PTSD or Battle Fatigue.

Traumatic Brain Injuries are closely identified with the wars in the Middle East and the powerful IEDs used there. With the development of these high-tech explosives that have made their way into the war zone, the destructiveness of bombs, artillery shells, and roadside IEDs has increased dramatically. Soldiers, who in past wars would have been killed by these tremendous blasts, now survive, due to the development and fielding of a new generation of body armor. These soldiers show very few outward signs of injury and, following a battle or bombing incident, are often overlooked by medics who are rushing to treat those with obvious blood wounds. The soldier with a mild or moderate TBI is often quickly returned to duty or, at best, given light duty for a few days and then returned to normal duty.

An example of someone who received this type of injury is Marine Sgt. Robert Reed who, while serving in Iraq, was involved in at least four bombing incidents, none of which caused any visible injuries. Reed was able to complete his deployment and return to the States with his unit. But a year after he left Iraq, he's still trying to understand and cope with his wounds. Reed was finally diagnosed with TBI, from the serious damage caused by the explosive blasts that rattled his brain on four different occasions.

Due to the nature of the wars in Afghanistan and particularly Iraq, with no frontlines and an enemy that roams at will, placing IEDs along virtually every roadway, TBIs are occurring on a regular basis. This type of warfare is causing thousands of these injuries every year, and military and naval medical experts are experimenting with different techniques to try to develop programs that will better identify and treat these injuries.

A secondary injury associated with TBI is the constant anxiety of living and working in an area where these huge explosions occur on a daily basis. After one of these terrorist attacks, the service members who arrive on the scene to secure and clean up the area are often traumatized by the utter destruction and scattered body parts that they are forced to observe and collect. Many of these individuals will carry those images in their minds for prolonged periods of time and some will eventually wind up as Battle Fatigue or psychological casualties.

Although many TBI symptoms are the same as PTSD, the injuries are usually more serious to a soldier's physical rather than his psychological health. Often misdiagnosed as PTSD, TBI can lead to a variety of disabilities such as memory loss, emotional instability, and problems with balance, vision and hearing. Reed, the returning veteran, suffers from dizzy spells and double vision. His injuries have seriously distorted his sense of direction. Once he enjoyed hiking in the woods for hours without a compass. Now he needs a GPS device to get around town. Previously, he was able to finish his college homework assignments in only a few minutes. Now he toils for hours after his classes at the University of Utah. "I always had a quick mind and good memory, but now I forget the simplest things," Reed said, in slow measured sentences. "My memory is so bad that, at times, I have to take out my billfold to see where I live."

Part of the reason why so many soldiers are not diagnosed at the time, has to do with the nature of this war. Typically, a vehicle carrying four to twelve men or women is traveling on a road and is hit by an IED. The vehicle is destroyed, and two or three soldiers are seriously wounded. The medics quickly arrive, and as they are trained to do, the person who is senior in rank sends the apparently uninjured soldiers out to form a protective perimeter for the injured soldiers and their damaged vehicle. When the evacuation helicopter arrives, only those soldiers who have blood injuries are usually evacuated. All the others, mainly because of a high level of adrenalin that keeps them alert and able to perform their duties, are assumed to be uninjured. Usually, no record is kept of those soldiers who were involved in the incident, and as each goes his own way and the adrenalin starts to wear off, the incident is placed in the back of everyone's minds and quickly forgotten. Later, soldiers begin to develop slight symptoms. For Robert Reed, it was dizzy spells and double vision.

In a recent interview at Fort Hood, Texas, psychiatrist Hemant Thakur, who has treated TBIs in Iraq and currently at the VA Medical Center in Kansas City, stated, "Many of these patients look fine. They have impairment, but it's not necessarily obvious."

Thakur once questioned a soldier in Iraq who appeared to be uninjured after a blast. The doctor asked him, referring to his rifle, "What is this?" "A rifle!" responded the soldier. "What do you do with it?" he asked. "I don't know," the soldier responded. Another soldier under Thakur's care, while returning from Iraq, landed at Dulles International Airport and got into two fistfights. Upon arrival home, he cursed at his mother and used such foul language toward his girlfriend that she left him. The soldier's mother told Thakur that her son had never gotten into fights or cursed before.

"Here's a man who looks physically OK (no outward signs of injury). But he is not whole." Dr. Thakur reported that, as of January 2007, the military's medical system has treated more than five thousand troops for TBI, and this does not reflect the large number who didn't seek treatment for their wounds. Based on surveys of returning soldiers and Marines, the number suffering from this condition may be significantly higher than these figures indicate. The surveys, some as recent as April 2008, indicate that as high as 15–25 percent of troops posted to combat zones in Iraq and Afghanistan reported suffering one or more concussions. About 19 percent of these veterans of Iraq and Afghanistan who were screened by the VA tested positive for TBI symptoms.

Based on a 2007 study of soldiers returning to Fort Carson, Colorado, the number of soldiers with TBI symptoms army-wide could be as high as four hundred thousand and growing daily. "We have a large population who have suffered injuries," said Jason Forrester, the advocacy group's policy director. "You have these soldiers coming back with behavioral problems. They haven't been adequately screened, and they haven't gotten treatment."

As of June 2007, service members get battlefield screenings for concussions and, at the end of their deployments, they answer yes/no questionnaires that are designed to identify medical problems, including TBIs. At the same time, any soldier applying to the VA for treatment is screened for TBIs. This is a fine beginning, but one of the injuries that occur with TBIs is a loss of memory, so most of these soldiers being interviewed do not recall IED incidents. Ironically, the ones who screened positive for PTSD were the least likely to seek help for fear of being stigmatized.

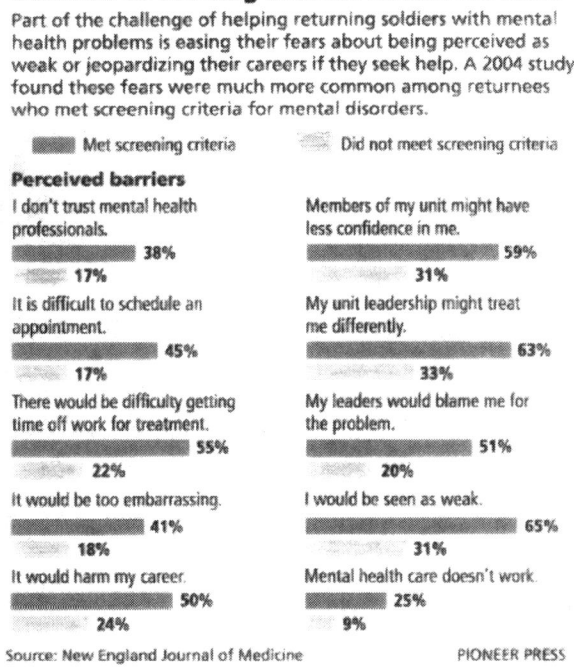

Barriers to seeking mental health services
Part of the challenge of helping returning soldiers with mental health problems is easing their fears about being perceived as weak or jeopardizing their careers if they seek help. A 2004 study found these fears were much more common among returnees who met screening criteria for mental disorders.

■ Met screening criteria   ▨ Did not meet screening criteria

Perceived barriers

I don't trust mental health professionals.
■ 38%
▨ 17%

Members of my unit might have less confidence in me.
■ 59%
▨ 31%

It is difficult to schedule an appointment.
■ 45%
▨ 17%

My unit leadership might treat me differently.
■ 63%
▨ 33%

There would be difficulty getting time off work for treatment.
■ 55%
▨ 22%

My leaders would blame me for the problem.
■ 51%
▨ 20%

It would be too embarrassing.
■ 41%
▨ 18%

I would be seen as weak.
■ 65%
▨ 31%

It would harm my career.
■ 50%
▨ 24%

Mental health care doesn't work.
■ 25%
▨ 9%

Source: New England Journal of Medicine   PIONEER PRESS

Col. Paul D. Walker (Ret)

As mentioned earlier, after a combat incident occurs and those with blood injuries are removed from the scene, those who were only shaken by the blast and just display momentary symptoms are returned to duty. This is what you would expect from good soldiers. They want to stay with their unit and continue performing their duties; anything less would be letting their buddies down.

Getting back to Robert Reed, back in 2006, he was stationed in Anbar Province, West of Baghdad, where his unit was rebuilding schools and hospitals. Then, just two months into his tour, Reed was traveling between local towns when a remote-controlled bomb exploded under his Humvee, but no one was seriously injured. Due to the nature of the "hit-and-run" type of fighting in this area, he was later involved in two more, similar roadside attacks. Following each of the incidents, Reed was examined by the unit medic and put on light duty for a day or so and then returned to normal work.

These injuries began to take a toll on him and, after the second blast, he noticed that his eyes would cross when he tried to read. "Anything with a repeat pattern would cause my eyes to go crazy—going down stairs, Venetian blinds, etc." His memory suffered, and he had trouble following directions. Finally, in August of 2006, while Reed was on a foot patrol, a makeshift bomb exploded less than thirty feet away. This was a powerful explosion that ripped through cars and hit civilians, but the Marines were spared.

"I was wearing body armor, but the shock wave was so powerful, it knocked me down," Reed said. He was hospitalized for two days and has no recollection of the events. From this point forward, Reed's dizziness and memory got steadily worse. "Everyone noticed me stumbling around and falling down. I was also jumbling my words, and my speech was slurred." With his disabilities now becoming obvious and no procedures in place for treating these types of injuries, Reed's chain of command allowed him to finish out the remainder of his tour within the protection of the base camp.

Recent sports-medicine research into the harm that concussions can cause football players when they resume play too soon, has also heightened the military's awareness about the seriousness of head injuries, reports

LTC Michael Jaffee, director of the Defense and Veterans Brain Injury Center. "We are much more diligent at identifying mild injuries and concussions," he said.

"Brain injuries caused by explosions may differ considerably from injuries caused by striking the head," reports Douglas Ambrose, a psychiatrist and the acting chief of staff at the VA Medical Center. "Blast injuries tend to affect many parts of the brain. That's why troops with TBIs may experience a number of subtle handicaps. You may not have somebody with a skull fracture or any other obvious physical injury, yet there's damage to the brain," Ambrose said. "And that tissue doesn't heal itself very well."

The Army currently has a pilot program to test soldiers' mental skills and establish a baseline, before they are deployed to Iraq so doctors can better assess the effects of TBIs. This is real progress but slow in coming. For at least forty years, the armed forces has given each of its new pilots a brain scan or EEG. This is also done to establish a baseline so that, in the event of an accident or crash, medical personnel can determine if there has been injury to the brain. With the cost of long-term care going up dramatically, the military should establish a baseline for each of its service members, to provide better and more effective care.

In January 2008, the 101st Airborne Division deployed to Afghanistan and took with them sensor lined helmets that could prove to be vital in assessing the impact from blasts, roadside bombs and other incidents that can cause TBI. About half of the "Screaming Eagles" were issued these sensor lined helmets upon deployment, and the remainder received them a few months later. Soldiers of the 4th Infantry Division have also received helmets with sensors. The hope is that the data gathered from these sensors will assist the army in treating TBIs and in improving the helmets as well as other protective equipment issued to soldiers prior to deployments. The sensors will gather data about impacts, ranging from a helmet that is dropped or kicked, to the impact caused by a motor vehicle accident, to a weapon firing nearby or the impact caused by an explosion. The primary reason for equipping soldiers with these advanced helmets is to measure the intensity of explosions. This will become a tremendous diagnostic tool, enabling medical personnel to know before a soldier even arrives from the field, if there is a possibility

Col. Paul D. Walker (Ret)

of a TBI and thus allowing doctors to prepare appropriate medical care. The U.S. Department of Defense has just recently begun to coordinate with the VA in developing guidelines for these devices and others in treating TBIs for all the armed services.

New Helmet Sensors Will Measure Blast Impact

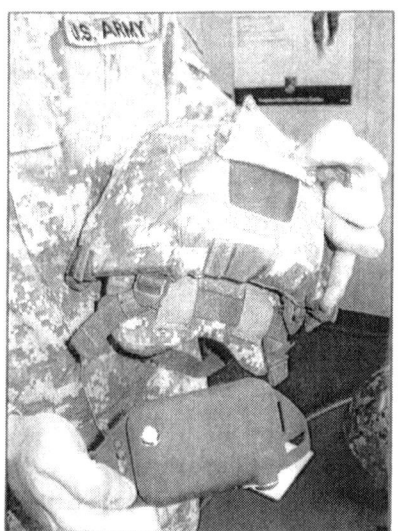

The U.S. Army's Program Executive Office Soldier pushed the concept of a helmet-mounted sensor able to collect blast data from concept to fielding in a record six months. The 101st Airborne Division is receiving the sensors before its deployment to Afghanistan. Photo by Donna Miles

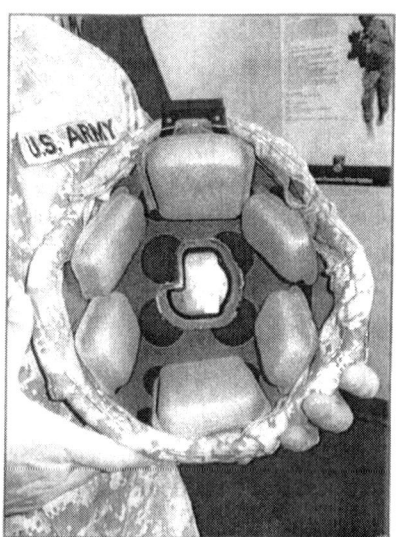

The 4th Infantry Division will receive an internally mounted helmet sensor before its deployment to Iraq this fall. Photo by Donna Miles

The face of Battle Fatigue is certainly not a simple one, and health care professionals have recently discovered that those suffering from PTSD often have the symptoms of TBI, and in many cases, the reverse is true.

Chapter Two

The Hidden Casualties Among Us: A Short History

This chapter will take a historical look at various individuals who have suffered from Battle Fatigue, how it has changed their lives, and the steps they or local commanders could have taken to reduce these injuries.

The vibrant history of the American people is often measured by events directly related to their wars. Starting with conflicts involving early settlers and Native Americans in the original thirteen colonies, each violent episode left in its wake, a small population of veterans suffering from Battle Fatigue.

As discussed earlier, the six most common symptoms of those suffering from Battle Fatigue are insomnia, recurring nightmares, flashbacks, isolation, a need to be armed, and a constant search for danger and risk.

It comes as a surprise to most of us that these symptoms were present in one of the earliest and most widely known figures in American history—Daniel Boone. Following a brief period of service in the colonial militia, Boone virtually abandoned civilized society to live on the dangerous frontier.

The French and Indian war was fought to resolve a dispute involving France and England over who owned the land between the thirteen colonies and the Mississippi River. During the course of this war, Indian tribes were pressed into service by both sides, with rewards given for scalps taken. It was a particularly brutal war, fought mostly in the wild and unsettled land that would one day become known as the American Midwest.

Born in 1734, Boone took an active part in the French and Indian War, serving as a guide on Gen. Braddock's ill-fated expedition into western Pennsylvania. On this campaign, Boone witnessed the ambush and vicious slaughter of most of Braddock's force by tomahawk-wielding, bloodthirsty Indians. Boone was with George Washington who, after his disaster at Fort Necessity, had been brought back into service as a colonel to advise Braddock on the movement of troops through the wilderness areas of the colonies. Washington had advised the general against moving a large body of troops through such a confined area, but his advice was ignored. Positioned at the back of the column with the rear guard, Boone and Washington were together when the ambush was sprung. There was a horrible bloodbath as the Indians swarmed among the British soldiers, slaughtering almost the entire command. In the midst of this confusion, Washington was able to gather several men around him and fight a brutal "hand-to-hand" retreat to the rear. Covered with Indian blood and suffering from minor wounds, he and Boone were among the few who were able to escape. Both witnessed unspeakable violence and horror, Washington never mentioned the experience, and it seemed not to have affected him in later years, but in Boone's case, it colored the remainder of his life. Many believe that this experience with Gen. Braddock is what caused Boone to abandon the safe and reasonably secure life in the colonies and embark on the reckless career of a frontiersman. There, on the edges of civilization, he would spend the remainder of his eighty-six years roaming the unsettled Western lands, with the constant threat of danger always nearby, trying to recapturing the combat high he'd once known. Here, serious injury and death were often just a short step away and, although Boone was captured by hostile Indians on numerous occasions, he always managed a desperate, last-minute escape. However, three of his children and two of his brothers were not so fortunate. Boone finished his long life in a small log cabin on the edge of the Missouri Territory, where the frontier had then moved. It was there, living alone with his trusty rifle by his side, that Daniel Boone struggled with his demons, right up to the end.

The American Civil War was a period of transition for the U.S. military. The tactics used by both sides were those developed by Napoleon, half a century before. Weapons, on the other hand, represented new technology, and they dramatically changed the dynamics of warfare. During Napoleon's time, soldiers were armed with smooth-bore muskets that were accurate out to 25–50 yards. This allowed commanders to move units around the battlefield in massed formations and attack in close order, without the danger of suffering huge losses. However, new technology, developed just prior to the Civil War, changed all this and allowed gun manufacturers to produce more precise parts and to turn out gun barrels with deep rifling for greater accuracy. This new manufacturing technology now allowed rifles to fire with fine precision out to four hundred yards and artillery to fire with more deadly accuracy out to several thousand yards. The destructiveness of war was increased on both sides, as they employed outdated tactics that called for dense formations with soldiers equipped with new modern weapons. Casualties were extremely heavy, and wounds produced by the new "mini-balls" were ghastly. If a bone was struck by one of these new "slugs," it usually meant the amputation of a limb to save the soldier's life.

The armies of the north and south engaged in 2261 battles, which produced over 1 million casualties, more than all other American wars combined. Although no records were kept, and the exact number of Battle Fatigue casualties in this war is unknown, it is easy to see that the increase in violence and destructiveness also brought with it an increase in the number of soldiers who suffered psychological damage from the effects of this new type of warfare.

From letters sent home and journals kept by many soldiers, it's clear that the Civil War's close-fought combat did produce an unusually large number of these tormented souls, who, in order to escape the nightmares of the killing fields such as Cold Harbor and Gettysburg, headed west. There, many found healing and peace, living among the

Indians and wild animals on the fringes of civilization. John Wesley Powell, the one-armed, former Union Army major who explored the Colorado River, and the sergeant depicted in the movie *Dances with Wolves*, typify these weary, adventure-seeking veterans.

During World War I, American soldiers huddling in the muddy trenches of France were often subjected to massed artillery attacks that lasted for days or weeks and usually pulverized the safety of their defensive lines. The stress and anxiety caused by these attacks and the expectation of waiting to be blown to bits was too much for many of these exhausted men, and they simply stopped functioning as normal human beings. This was the first war where the psychological condition of Battle Fatigue was officially recognized and given a name: shell-shocked. The treatment, at the time, was geared toward getting soldiers back in the lines as soon as possible, whether they were cured or not.

Field hospitals of the day attempted very primitive techniques to desensitize these injured soldiers, such as hollering commands at close range or simulating the sounds of artillery landing close-by. Slapping was also tried, and generally patients were handled with a great deal of suspicion, that symptoms were being faked to avoid the trenches.

When the author was growing up in southwest Missouri during the late 1940s, there were many stories about a "crazy," disfigured World War I veteran who lived in the nearby Mark Twain National Forest. This pitiful old man avoided all contact with other human beings and would even climb a tree rather than come face-to-face with anyone. Deer hunters often reported finding his campsites and catching a glimpse of a ghostlike figure as he disappeared off in the distance. When concerned Forest Service officials finally tried to help him by literally capturing him with a net, he pleaded with them like a cornered animal, to just be left alone and not bothered. Unrecognized at the time, but undoubtedly from his conduct and war record, the man was suffering from some form of Battle Fatigue.

In World War II, Battle Fatigue was again studied, and those who suffered from it were recognized in aid stations as legitimate casualties. Some treatment was even provided to those suffering from it. However, the slapping incident involving Patton still indicated the widespread lack of understanding in the U.S. Military, for any form of Battle Fatigue and for those suffering from it.

Because America had been at peace, when the events that started World War II occurred, the entire nation was traumatized. The United States was caught almost totally unprepared and vulnerable when the Japanese struck Pearl Harbor. However, this attack did more than any other event to unify the nation in a common purpose to defeat Japan in any way it could. Interviews with America's "Greatest Generation," those who endured the Great Depression and World War II, always mention Pearl Harbor as a defining moment in their lives. This event caused them to come together as a people, to share the toil and sacrifice needed to win against a treacherous enemy. Then, following the war, this event served as a common bond for all Americans, and most were filled with a confidence that, after defeating two brutal enemies, there wasn't anything that they or the United States of America couldn't accomplish.

Now, almost seventy years later, many of those original survivors of that sneak attack are still very much alive and still wrestling with the trauma that it produced. Every year, dozens of these graying veterans make their way back to Hawaii to look upon the quiet waters of Pearl Harbor and remember their fallen comrades.

Recently, a group of these returning veterans was interviewed by *Modern Maturity* magazine. One, a sailor named Sterling R. Cale, vividly remembers, four days after the attack, boarding the shattered USS Arizona in command of a burial detail. For over sixty years, he had never been able to speak about his experiences on that day, but his mind had never let him forget. In September 2000, he could finally bear to write down what had happened: "The sight completely overwhelmed me, and I became nauseated and sick to my stomach. Little piles of ashes were in neat piles surrounding the antiaircraft guns. The ladder going into the fire control tower was packed solid with charred bodies, which were about three feet long and charred together so that a whole person was individually unrecognizable. In trying to 'spud' the bodies apart, the head, arms, legs, or some other part of a torso would come off or fall apart."

Battle Fatigue

Other veterans related how Pearl Harbor ghosts can pop up unexpectedly. When one man cut himself shaving and saw the water in the sink turn red, he remembered the blood-tinted waters of the harbor. A man whose father returned home stinking of gasoline after the attack, remembers December 7 whenever he smells gas fumes while filling his car. Rear Admiral Bernard Clarey had mixed emotions when he was called upon to welcome Japanese submarines to Pearl Harbor in 1963, stating that seeing the Rising Sun "suddenly brought back all the events of December 7, 1941." Ike Stutton, who ferried the wounded from the harbor to the infirmary, still wakes up screaming from nightmares in which he sees the faces of men who died while he was filling his launch with other victims before heading for Hospital Point.

Although the Philippine islands were attacked within hours of Pearl Harbor, the Japanese invasion there and the following heroic campaign by U.S. and Filipino forces on the Bataan peninsula are seldom mentioned in our schools or by public officials in their annual patriotic speeches commemorating the start of World War II.

The survivors of Bataan will tell you with a peculiar smile that their country abandoned them to their fate. Then, with anger in their voices, they will explain that, although their part of the war, like Pearl Harbor, started with a sneak attack, the struggle for the Philippines actually lasted over four months. During this time, the men were repeatedly told that help was on the way and were promised more food, ammunition, and reinforcements, if they would just hold out a little bit longer. Surrounded by the Japanese, with ammunition running out and casualties mounting, these ill-equipped, malnourished soldiers, most suffering from malaria, watched as their commanding general, Douglas MacArthur, ran out on them. Supposedly, he was too valuable to be captured by the Japanese.

The promises of "help is on the way" continued right up to the end, as these unfortunate warriors continued to battle with rusty, antiquated weapons, surviving on less than one thousand calories a day, much of it in the form of monkeys, iguana, and snakes gathered from the jungle.

On April 9, 1942, these half-starved and totally exhausted men had held out as long as they could and finally surrendered. It was the largest surrender in U.S. history. Next began the infamous sixty-five-mile Bataan Death March to prisoner-of-war camps. On this march, the cruel and sadistic nature of the Japanese soldiers would be revealed, as sick and exhausted men were casually executed for trivial infractions. Over six hundred Americans and well over ten thousand Filipinos lost their lives on this march.

When the American's surrendered on Bataan, the Japanese had expected approximately 30,000 prisoners of War to care for; instead, double or triple that number marched into captivity. Research following the war has revealed that, upon learning about the high number of POWs, the Japanese senior leadership issued orders to their forward units to reduce these numbers. Soldiers guarding the long columns of POWs responded by executing anyone who "fell out of the march" or was too sick to continue. In other words the weak were eliminated.

Survivors of this hellish captivity tell painfully traumatic stories of seeing friends tortured and beheaded, of having to bury comrades for lack of the most basic medicines, and of being treated in a brutal and ruthless manner by their fiendish guards. One of the survivors saw nine of his fellow prisoners shot because one man tried to escape. The doomed men dug their own pit, then kneeled by the edge and waited for the executioner to shoot them in the back of the head, dropping them one by one into a shared grave.

"For three years, we were always living on the edge there," said survivor Richard Gordon, "wondering what they were going to do to us, where the next beating would come from. I don't think there's a man who went through that experience who doesn't have some sort of psychological scarring; that certainly includes me. It takes a permanent bite out of you."

"It has been said that Bataan was a dress rehearsal for Vietnam. Certainly, the experience there offered important lessons about military preparedness, overextension, and commitment, which the planners in Vietnam seem generally to have ignored. As in Vietnam, the Bataan men found themselves fighting against an extremely foreign enemy in unfamiliar jungles of tropical Asia, waging a battle that was doomed to fail. And, as with Vietnam soldiers, the men of Bataan had to return home with a certain unspoken stigma, the awkward status of having lost or surrendered. Many of the syndromes and illnesses that have come to be associated with Vietnam veterans were suffered twenty-five years earlier by the American captives of the Japanese: insomnia, nightmares, and night sweats, bouts of profound depression, various mysterious symptoms that VA hospital doctors were reluctant to diagnose and treat—all the hallmarks of the condition now known as post-traumatic stress disorder but then not dignified with a name" (*Modern Maturity*, November 2001, p. 53).

As the final insult, after enduring the horrors of their four-month siege, the Death March, and over three years of deadly captivity, these men were not prepared to experience the awkward readjustment to normal civilian life after the war. Virtually all experienced difficulties, and most could not shake their past, as nightmares and feelings of guilt plagued them. In the first few years after the war, many of these courageous survivors, unable to return to a normal life, tried to self-medicate and died of alcoholism, or they suffered from depression and various combinations of residual chronic illnesses related to their captivity.

The experience of the Bataan survivors was not unique; most American POWs of World War II came home to find no parades or cheering crowds, no military or veterans' support, and no one interested or sympathetic to the sacrifices they had made. What they did find in many cases were girlfriends who had met someone else and had forgotten them, or wives who had gotten divorces and had married someone else. Those wives and girlfriends who had waited patiently for their men to return found that they were strangers with nothing in common. Those returning soldiers with children often found that the kids didn't remember them and wanted nothing to do with them. Old friends had moved on or had no way of understanding what the POWs had been through and didn't know what to say to them and so avoided or shunned them.

Some of the POWs couldn't break their old prisoner-of-war habits. They would steal food in restaurants or get arrested for shoplifting. Many would self-medicate to help them forget or to be able to sleep at night. Unfortunately, many of these men tried to run away from their lives and, when that didn't work, attempted suicide. The army and veterans administration, at the time, just didn't understand that these men needed special care. The policy was, very much, a "hands-off" approach to care.

There is a very sad story of men who had been ordered to surrender in the Philippines, who were brutalized by their captives and then shipped to Japan, to work in coal mines near Nagasaki. These U.S. soldiers were kept in the most despicable conditions imaginable, starved, degraded, and worked like animals. They lived in constant fear of death. Soon after Nagasaki was bombed, the gates of the prison were thrown open, and many of these scrappy men who had managed to survive on the edge of death for three-and-a-half years, commandeered public transportation, then made their way to the closest harbor and flagged down nearby U.S. ships. Within days of their release, most of these men had somehow managed to return to the United States without any sort of rehabilitation. Upon their arrival, they went directly home and found many of the situations described above. Most were disappointed at the kind of homecoming they received, and most turned to liquor, drugs, whores, and finally to suicide. They had endured so much and their anticipations were so great that there is no way that what they experienced when they arrived home could have lived up to what they had expected.

As a veteran of Vietnam who harbors mild feelings that his country turned its back on those who fought there, I cannot even begin to imagine the extreme feelings of anger and abandonment that must have overwhelmed the survivors of the Philippines.

During World War II, America's Eighth Air Force learned a great deal about stress and just how much a man could withstand on the highly dangerous missions over Nazi-occupied Europe. Flight crews assigned to the air force faced death and injury from a dozen different directions. On a typical mission, which might involve hundreds of B-17 bombers, each carrying a ten-man crew, it was just expected that a certain number of the bomb-loaded planes would be lost to accidents. Antiaircraft fire along the way and over the target would also take its toll and, finally, enemy fighter planes would usually intercept the flights going out and coming back. It is also important to remember that, at this point in the evolution of flight, just getting into a plane and taking off had its dangers. Add to this, the perils of combat, and the risks skyrocket.

After crews realized the odds against them, unit morale became an important issue to deal with. To solve the problem of having crews fly numerous missions while exposing themselves repeatedly to these dangers, the air force came up with a solution to keep these men at their battle stations and flying. Crews were told that, after twenty-five missions, they would be sent back to the States and assigned to safer duty. What they didn't tell them was that, statistically, a crew could only expect to survive a maximum of fifteen missions before being shot down.

While racking-up their twenty-five missions and being subjected to the stresses of combat, many crew members began exhibiting symptoms of very serious illnesses, both mental and physical. But when these overworked warriors reported to the flight surgeon or unit psychiatrist and started listing their symptoms, such as extreme tension, nervousness, or an inability to sleep, doctors would often tell them that, if they were sane enough to recognize that they had a problem, then they were sane enough to keep flying. The doctors would then give the airmen a small box of aspirin or cough syrup and send them back to their units as fit for duty. This contradiction became known as "Catch-22." Approximately thirty-three thousand airmen were lost on these missions over occupied Europe, and many of those who did make it home after their twenty-five missions or at the end of the war were never quite the same.

As stated earlier, during World War II the medical community finally became more professional in recognizing, diagnosing, and treating psychological injuries. Their motivation generally was, and correctly should have been, to treat the soldier, so that, as in World War I, he could be quickly returned to his unit, which often meant a trip back to the front lines.

When the movie *Saving Private Ryan* first came out, journalists, in search of a good story, would often take a group of World War II veterans, who had participated in the Normandy Landings, to see it and record their reactions. For many of these graying veterans, the first fifteen minutes of the movie suddenly brought back to life the haunting terrors of long ago, and they bolted from the theatre. Apparently, these members of the Greatest Generation were still struggling with unresolved issues of Battle Fatigue.

After the war, young pilots of the American Volunteer Group, better known as "The Flying Tigers," chose another method to relieve their Battle Fatigue symptoms; they formed the "Hell's Angels" motorcycle club. Then, for the next decade, these fearless veterans attempted to recapture the adrenaline rush of aerial combat by racing their big Harleys over the back roads of America.

One of the most famous and widely known cases of Battle Fatigue from World War II comes from a most unlikely individual, Maj. Dick Winters of the book, "Band of Brothers." The book follows the wartime experiences of a unique company in the 101st Airbourne Division that participated in every major battle of the European War. Under Winters' leadership, this company took part in the war's most extreme combat and accomplished every mission with minimum losses, while causing the greatest damage to the enemy. The unit's success, was due in no small part, to the soldiers looking out for each other like brothers. After the war and for the next 50 years, they continued to stay in touch and were a support group to each other.

Returning home after the war, this battle-hardened leader of the Band of Brothers was attempting to re-enter civilian life and the slower pace of life, when he began to experience the symptoms of a letdown. The following example illustrates this process of deprogramming. While Winters was out one morning enjoying a quiet walk in his hometown, a young boy passed him on the sidewalk and dragged a stick across a picket fence, sending Winters diving into the gutter. He momentarily thought he was back in combat and under enemy fire. "I picked myself up out of the gutter," he later recalled. "There was no thought; it was all reaction. You're still tight. You're still fighting the dammed war, and that was a machine gun" (Biggest Brother, P217 Larry Alexander, NAL, Caliber 2005).

After his release from the military, Winters found himself withdrawing from others and losing all respect for men who had not served. He continued to wear his uniform long after he'd been discharged. Years later, Winters referred to this period as a very bitter time for him. He missed his army friends and had great difficulty sleeping at home in his own bed. He was mentally exhausted, had no job and no direction for his life, and allowed his mind to wander back to the dark events that had occurred during the war. Part of this new adjustment was to understand that he was no longer in–charge, no longer giving orders, and no longer carrying the heavy burden of responsibility. When friends came to visit, he refused to see them. Finally, after a period of months, Winters "found himself" and began a more normal life of job, family, church, and social activities. After examining Winters's successful experience in returning to a "normal" life following his horrible wartime experiences (horrible may not be the correct word to describe his experiences—"extreme" or "intense" might be more appropriate), several advantages stand out: he was older than those he had served with and he was a nondrinker and did not resort to self-medication as so many did. He also eventually forced himself to interact socially with others, and he maintained contact with his friends from the war.

Iwo Jima was the most heavily fortified island of World War II and when the Marines came ashore they were greeted by a murderous fire from 1,500 hidden bunkers, each one containing at least two heavy machineguns. The fanatical defenders had also zeroed in the beaches with hundreds of artillery pieces and the killing never let up.

Unloading from a giant American fleet of over 800 warships, three Marine divisions of over 70,00 men, the largest Marine force ever assembled under one commander, made the deadly amphibious assault. To cover these landings, the navy had laid down a rolling barrage of the type not seen since World War I. But it was quickly apparent to the frontline Marines that the intense bombardment had simply failed to destroy or even weaken the defenders. All along the two-mile beachhead Japanese defenders emerged from their hidden positions and began to take a heavy toll of the attackers. An example of the emotional horrors that greeted the Marines was a childhood memory recalled by Lieutenant Keith Wells as he waded ashore. "He was griped by the same nervous fear and anticipation he had witness among the cattle at his father's slaughterhouse, as the doors would close behind the terrified animals and they were herded up the chute." By the end of the first day, the Marines had secured most of their objectives but they had paid a heavy price.

Okinawa was even more costly than Iwo Jima. Approaching the size of the Normandy Invasion with 1,200 ships and over 180,000 troops this operation claimed the lives of approximately 13,000 Americans, including the 4 star commanding general and produced over 26,000 Battle Fatigue casualties. The number of psychological injuries was so large that a special hospital was opened just to treat these patients. Okinawa would produce the most and worst cases of Battle Fatigue of the entire war.

Korea and Vietnam were similar in many ways. Both were fought during the Cold War, both made major efforts to contain the conflicts, and victory for American forces was ruled out. The wars were unpopular both with the American people and with the soldiers who fought them. In the case of Korea, almost sixty years after our initial commitment, U.S. forces are still there, attempting to maintain the *status quo*. Vietnam, the first televised war, even with the protest fever of the 1960s was still very similar to Korea. The primary difference was a lack of a national will to remain for any prolonged period of time, as we had done in Korea. The subsequent takeover of the South by North Vietnam called into question for many veterans, the value of their service. Returning veterans who suffered from Battle Fatigue, often bitterly complained that their government had unfairly singled them out to shoulder the burden of service, while allowing so many others to stay home.

With the nation's long history of wars and psychological injuries, Battle Fatigue training for regular combat line officers is still the same today as it was for previous wars—nonexistent. This, despite the fact that, with additional training, units could be more efficient, the men more productive, and the burden on society to care for the "silent casualties" greatly reduced.

Since it is viewed as purely a medical problem, military leaders today assume that, if the personnel in a unit are going to be subjected to conditions that will produce Battle Fatigue, then the battalion surgeon or medical officer will warn the commander. In actual practice, this rarely happens. Part of the problem is the military tradition of placing the mission first, and the health and welfare of the troops is secondary. All commanders realize that, in accomplishing their mission, soldiers will often be killed or wounded; that's the nature of their business. Acknowledging this, it's still very possible to limit the length of time that soldiers are exposed to intense combat. Today in the Middle East, the experience is much the same as it was in Vietnam, and many feel that by sending in an occupying force that was too small for the mission, our senior leadership caused many soldiers and units to be exposed to intense combat longer than was medically acceptable for healthy soldiers.

A memoir about my service in Vietnam was published a few years ago. Then, within a few months of its publication, several former soldiers that I had served with read the book, and old memories, some good, some bad, were stirred up, and they decided to contact me. The conversations were often emotional, and in the course of one long session, a former tank commander, Sergeant Roscoe Smith, told me that my old driver, a soldier named Becker, was being treated for PTSD and seemed to be in failing health. I recalled that Becker had been an excellent driver and had done his part on the various details without complaining. He had been quiet and had kept pretty much to himself. I do recall, on two different occasions, finding him off by himself, crying over the loss of close friends. So, I was not too surprised to hear that he was having trouble putting his combat experiences behind him. Aware that sometimes very intense or traumatic experiences can stay submerged in a person's mind for many years and that talking about these experiences can sometimes be helpful, I asked Sergeant Smith if he would get Becker's phone number so I could call him.

In a few days, Sergeant Smith called me with Becker's address in Louisiana and a relative's phone number. He indicated that Becker had been hard to find because he'd moved around a great deal. After several unsuccessful attempts to reach him and after leaving messages in various places, a woman with a very frail voice called me one afternoon and said she was Becker's sister. She wanted to know if her brother was in some sort of trouble. I explained who I was and that I was just trying to reach her brother to find out how he was getting along. In a guarded way, she explained that her brother was very sick with an addiction problem and had been for sometime. She went on to say that he'd been in and out of several jobs over the years and had even spent time in prison. After a long pause, she told me that he'd just never quite gotten over what he'd seen in Vietnam. I asked her if a phone call from me would be helpful or if it would just make things worse. She let me know that a call from his old platoon leader couldn't make him any worse, and it might actually help. Indicating that she didn't have a phone number for him, she said her brother sometimes stopped by on Sundays for a hot meal, so if I wanted to speak with him, I should try to call back on a Sunday. This I agreed to do and the following Sunday, I called the sister again. After what seemed like several minutes, my old driver came on the phone and, in an upbeat and cheerful voice, said, "Lt. Walker, How's you doin'?" We talked for at least thirty minutes, mostly about what he'd been doing since the war. It seemed that he had moved all over the South, doing mostly gardening work in the summer and food service in the wintertime. Finally, I asked if he'd been able to put the war behind him.

After a long pause and in a slow and halting voice, he said, "Almost, but I still think about some of the things we saw over there." Then I told him about an old dream I had, about the enemy attacking while we were cleaning weapons. This prompted him to tell me about an incident that had bothered him the most. He began, "It was during the rainy season, and we was movin' around north of Lai Khe, in the rubber trees. The platoon was on line, and as we came out of a thicket of tall bushes, right there in front of us was a big bomb crater and back aways, at the foot of some stumpy trees, was three dead soldiers. As we got closer, you could see red ants and bugs all over the bodies. One of them bodies looked like the skull had been jerked out of his head. He was just lying there with his head collapsed, like a balloon with the air let out, his eyes wide open and teeth clenched in sort of a sick smile." Becker went on to say that he couldn't shake the picture of this enemy soldier out of his head and that virtually every night, unless he had a few drinks, this image, along with some others, tormented him and wouldn't let him sleep. I asked Becker if he was getting any help for his sleep problem and he indicated that he had gone to the VA several years ago, but nothing they did seemed to help.

To wrap up our long conversation, I told him about a reunion of our old outfit, the 1st Infantry Division, that was to be held soon in nearby Nashville, Tennessee. I told him I'd be there and urged him to attend and meet some of his old platoon buddies and that this might be good for him. I also promised to send him a copy of my book, with some information about the reunion. Becker didn't attend the reunion and, a few months later when I called his sister, she informed me that her brother had passed away. When I asked about the circumstances of his death; she would only say, in her tiny frail voice, that "after a weekend of heavy drinking, he had committed suicide."

Becker was further evidence of the different levels of stress and tolerances that soldiers can withstand before suffering serious damage to their minds.

As I recalled, the rainy season that Becker so vividly described, it was at the beginning of this miserable period that my tour of duty had begun. Out of college less than a year, I took over an armored cavalry platoon consisting of ten armored vehicles and sixty-eight men, including several experienced sergeants. As military operations commenced, and frequent contact was made with the enemy, casualties began to mount. Replacements did not come close to making up our losses, so by April of 1967, my platoon was down to thirty men, less than half of what we'd started with. From the standpoint of Battle Fatigue, the situation was ripe to produce casualties.

During the days of full manning, each vehicle had 4-7 men—four on the tanks and seven on the armored personnel carriers. This allowed the crews to pull a reasonable guard duty of one to two hours each night and to also provide men to the required listening posts and ambush patrols, while still permitting plenty of rest for the soldiers.

With reduced manning, the mission stayed the same, but the men received less sleep, and the stress factors and accidents went up dramatically.

Reduced manning also stretched the leadership or chain of command dangerously thin. There were fewer sergeants, so more things had to be done personally by the platoon leader and, because we were relying upon untrained and inexperienced vehicle commanders, more things had to be double and triple-checked.

It was during this time of limited manning, while pulling double shifts of guard duty and filling in for missing sergeants that my worst day occurred.

We were operating in an area where the enemy was reported to have hung personnel mines in trees, that would decapitate an entire crew as the vehicle passed nearby. On the previous day, I'd lost my new platoon sergeant when his tank hit a five-hundred-pound bomb buried in the middle of the road. The commotion created by this incident, with the grisly removal of bodies and the recovery of twisted vehicle parts, caused a cloud of despair to descend over the platoon.

At daybreak the next day, the platoon was clearing a rubber plantation road, when one of our scout vehicles stuck another mine and two men were killed and four wounded. The driver, a large man, was killed and his body was horribly mutilated. Due to his size and the condition of his body, it was difficult to remove him.

Later that day, as the armored column continued north, our unit was ordered to move off the road and investigate suspicious movement and sniper fire from a nearby tree line. As we pulled off the main road, a tremendous explosion ripped through the armored vehicle directly behind me, blowing it upside down, killing two and wounding three. As I raced back to the stricken vehicle and pulled the mutilated bodies from under the smoking wreck, two soldiers came up to me sobbing, saying that the vehicle driver, their friend, was still alive but trapped inside the smoking vehicle, and they couldn't get him out. Frantically walking around the smoking vehicle, I could smell the strong odor of raw gasoline and expected the gas tanks to explode at any moment. Finally, after weighing the odds, I grabbed a crowbar and pried open the inverted combat hatch in the rear. Then, with a fire extinguisher in one hand, I entered the smoke-filled compartment. Groping around, I found the unconscious driver and dragged him to safety.

This incident totally drained me of energy and for several days, I performed my duties as if moving in slow motion with no interest in anything except preserving the lives of as many of my soldiers as possible. I continued to serve as platoon leader for two additional months, but my enthusiasm and warrior spirit had been badly damaged. It took more than three years to completely recover emotionally from the trauma of that day.

Analyzing the events and circumstances of that sad day, it is apparent that physical and mental fatigue played a large role in the emotional damage that was done. The extreme violence and almost complete destruction of three of our armored vehicles without directly encountering the enemy, plus the gruesome mutilation of fellow soldiers, further increased this effect. Also, the fact that we were attacked by a hidden, invisible enemy added an element of apprehension, much like being caught in the middle of a minefield and being unable to protect oneself. In examining this incident, the factor that might be overlooked is that many of the men were at the end of their tours. The unit had been undermanned for at least two months with three men manning each vehicle while performing the same details and guard duty as before, but doing twice as much work. I am convinced that the extreme fatigue of the unit on this day contributed in no small way to the loss of lives and vehicles, plus it contributed to the deep Battle Fatigue injuries that were suffered later.

Vietnam veterans were given a strong voice by retired General Hal Moore with the publication of his book in 2008, *We Are Soldiers Still*. Prior to his return to Vietnam in October 1993, he states, "All along our war and our battles remained fresh in our memories and our nightmares. We had a lot of unfinished business that could only be conducted on those long-ago battlefields. We had old ghosts, old demons that tugged at hearts and minds and sent some of our comrades in search of a name for what ailed us, and help in dealing with that ailment".

"Years after our battles and our return home the Veterans Administration and its medical specialists put a name to a condition many of our Vietnam veterans experienced, posttraumatic stress disorder (PTSD), and began, belatedly, offering group therapy to help veterans deal with the condition."

Some of General Moore's men experienced psychological damage from too much exposure to intense combat and began to feel that "their number was up," or that they wouldn't be going home.

Those unfamiliar with combat might think that it is normal for individuals who have been exposed to intense combat to foresee their own deaths in battle. This is, in fact, not a normal reaction for healthy combat soldiers. The healthy ones are able to adjust and continue to believe that "the other guy is going to get it, not me." A soldier in good mental health does not think death is imminent and yet continue to function normally, with blind acceptance of his fate.

A brief passage from a memoir written by a surgeon who served on Iwo Jima helps explain the true feelings of healthy Marines. Expressing his thoughts about a recent newspaper article, he said, "Our Marines were willing to lay down their lives for their country? This statement was sheer nonsense, for the overwhelming majority of the men felt they would be spared, and that it was the next guy that would be killed or wounded. They had no intention of laying down their lives for their country or anything else. Each man believed he would be one of the lucky ones to return home. Those who lost or never did have this feeling of invulnerability would sooner or later crack up."

Another important factor to consider about those who have experienced prolonged exposure to combat is the necessary anxiety of adjustment to a less intense, normal civilian routine. Veterans of Afghanistan and Iraq are the latest examples of this difficult transition. While involved in an extended period of combat, as the mind and body protest, soldiers do adjust, to the "combat high" that becomes the norm. Then upon stand down, reassignment, or discharge, there is a tremendous letdown, and many service members find it difficult to adjust to the slower pace of a normal routine. Some who are unable to adjust to the slower pace seek out dangerous activities such as motorcycles, skydiving, car racing, or hang gliding, which allow them to recapture the "adrenaline rush" they had grown accustomed to in combat. A small percentage of these men spend the rest of their lives in pursuit of this combat high.

Kenneth Brown, who flew B-26s during World War II, provides the following observations about adjusting to civilian life: "Much has been written about the readjustment problems of combat veterans, and I have little to add. My war had been relatively clean and comfortable. Of necessity, however, it was often stressful and sometimes extremely violent. And that proved my biggest problem. After being in combat for some time, I truly became "hooked" on it, so much so that, when not in combat, it became difficult to find satisfaction from normal kinds of recreation. Reading, for example, was simply too dull. Even something like playing poker became less satisfying, compensated only by higher stakes, which were always climbing. When suddenly removed from combat entirely, I felt a real letdown, somewhat like a drug addict's withdrawal symptoms when quitting "cold turkey." In response to this, it is hardly surprising that some men become mercenaries, forever seeking whatever war is available, no matter where it is or whose side they are fighting on. These withdrawal symptoms may continue for many months, and they resemble the symptoms of drug withdrawal.

In past years, those in our society who suffered from Battle Fatigue did so mainly in silence, and mention of this condition rarely appeared in newspapers or in our daily conversations. Today, however, things have changed, due to the huge numbers of service members returning from the Middle East with psychological injuries. One can hardly pick up a newspaper or turn on a television without learning about the latest crisis involving those suffering from PTSD or Battle Fatigue. With this kind of publicity, those in the health care field are expecting to make great progress in diagnosing and treating this injury.

Now, with events in the Middle East grabbing most of the headlines, it is only on rare occasions that we still hear from soldiers of previous wars. One such story surfaced recently when a World War II veteran, who'd wrestled most of his life with terrors that had followed him from Guadalcanal, was listed on the FBI Ten Most Wanted Fugitives list. It seems that, for most of his life, he was just like anyone else in his neighborhood, but then in recent years, he began to change ever so slightly. He began to talk of the war and began to imagine that he was back in the jungles of Guadalcanal and that anyone who approached him was a Japanese soldier trying to kill him. On numerous occasions, not recognizing his wife, he had struggled with her and almost killed her. One evening, when the veteran was particularly wild and uncontrollable, his wife contacted a grown son who lived nearby to ask for his help in calming the father. The son complied and soon arrived at the father's home. In the meantime, the father had obtained a loaded pistol. When the son entered the father's room, he fired three shots, killing the son instantly. The father then fled the scene and, for over two years, has managed to elude police officers.

Newspapers covering the story eventually discovered that the father was being treated at the local veterans' hospital for Battle Fatigue and had been for many years. This prompted several articles about Battle Fatigue, and most emphasized the facts that there was no effective treatment program available and that those afflicted faced the hopeless prospects of a progressively deteriorating condition.

The hopeless prospects for treating this condition, as stated by the newspapers, was completely incorrect but certainly indicates the lack of understanding most people have of the illness and its treatment. There are a number of treatments now available, and their effectiveness will be discussed in a later chapter.

Since World War II, the medical community in our modern armed forces has learned to better identify and treat Battle Fatigue; however, it is still the senior military leadership who, by the way they manage the force and commit it to battle, are responsible for the large number of psychological casualties produced. This group must be educated about the conditions and circumstances that cause Battle Fatigue, if the numbers are ever going to be reduced significantly.

Chapter Three

The Story of George Barr

While doing research for this book, I came across a heartbreaking story of a young lieutenant who suffered from the worst case of Battle Fatigue that I've ever encountered and his truly remarkable recovery. The following is that soldier's story.

Each year on December 7, America remembers the "dastardly and unprovoked" attack on our Pacific Fleet at Pearl Harbor, which started World War II. But, as important as this occasion is, little is known of our very dramatic retaliation for this dark event that took place on April 18, 1942. On this date, Lt. Col. Jimmy Doolittle, commanding sixteen B-25 bombers, lifted off from the storm-swept decks of the USS Hornet, just 680 miles from the Japanese coast, to bomb the enemy capitol. Described as a suicide mission, Doolittle's Raiders, as they were called, consisted of eighty young men who raised the spirits of a nation at war and provided hope that the string of losses we'd suffered at the hands of a vicious enemy had finally come to an end. The "Doolittle Raid" was proof that the arsenal of democracy would eventually prevail.

The focus of this story is a Lt. George Barr, who was part of this courageous mission. As the war began, Barr was serving as a B-25 navigator with the Seventeenth Bomb Group, a unit that had been given the mission of patrolling the waters around Seattle, Washington, for enemy submarines.

In early January, this unit was unexpectedly transferred to South Carolina for submarine patrolling off the East Coast. En route to South Carolina, one squadron of sixteen planes, for unknown reasons at the time, was diverted to Minneapolis. There, the sixteen crews were brought together, and the squadron commander, CPT. Davey Jones, spoke to them in very serious terms. He explained that a special mission was being planned which would be "dangerous, important, and interesting." He further explained that only volunteers would be allowed to go. Despite repeated questions, the captain could tell them no more about the mission. He finished by saying "you've heard all the particulars I can give you. So, who'll volunteer?" He then added, "It's perfectly all right if you don't. It's strictly up to you." Remarkably, nearly every hand in the room went up, including George Barr's.

The volunteers and their planes were moved to Eglin Field, Florida, and secrecy quickly closed in around the men and their aircraft. At Eglin, the planes were modified by having their guns and radios removed, so that extra fuel tanks could be added for greater flying range. Then, since some of the planes were likely to fall into enemy hands, the Top-Secret Norden bombsights were also removed from the planes and replaced with simple rifle type sights.

As their training progressed, naval personnel were brought in to show the pilots how to get a fully loaded B-25 off the runway in five hundred feet or less. For navigators like George Barr, the squadron took long distance flights across the Gulf of Mexico to simulate long bombing missions. Then, to polish the art of not being detected, they would travel at fifty feet above the ocean, sweep up to bombing altitude, open the bomb bay doors and drop their practice dummies onto selected targets. It was a grueling schedule, in the air at 7 AM and often still flying at 10 PM.

On Tuesday, March 3, the pilots and crews were assembled in the small operations office and, for the first time, introduced to their commander. As the men waited in the cramped room and speculated about who the commander would be and why all the secrecy, suddenly the door opened and Lt. Col. Jimmy Doolittle strode to the front of the room and began addressing them. Those present were stunned that such a legendary figure would be assigned to this project. For most of their lives, they had heard about Doolittle's daring exploits to expand the frontiers of aviation, and now he was their leader. They now knew that this mission was going to be something big. When, at the end of his remarks, he said "if you have any doubts, drop out now," none of those present even remotely considered dropping out. The general feeling was that whatever Doolittle wanted them to do, as long as he was with them, they'd go ahead and do it without question.

On April 1, 1942, the squadron arrived at Alameda, California, and began loading their planes aboard the USS Hornet. Then, after all sixteen B-25s were secured to the flight deck, the carrier was moved to the middle of San Francisco Bay and anchored. The airmen were now called together and given a very serious security briefing about not discussing their aircraft, their training, or any possible mission with anyone, not even their wives or girlfriends, and that any breach of security would automatically eliminate them from the mission. Following this, Col. Doolittle announced that they would all be given one last night of shore leave that included the full range of pleasures that San Francisco had to offer.

Next morning, all were present aboard ship as the Hornet got underway and sailed under the Golden Gate Bridge. With San Francisco still in sight off the stern, Doolittle again called his men together and, for the first time, told them exactly what their mission would be. When he finished, he said, "If there are any of you who don't want to go, just tell me … because the chances of you making it back are pretty slim." Again, no one raised his hand or spoke up; all were fully committed to the mission.

Six days after the Hornet and her protective shield of cruisers and destroyers had departed San Francisco, Vice Adm. William Halsey left Pearl Harbor with a task force that included the carrier USS Enterprise. This task force would join the Hornet in mid-Pacific for the final run toward Japan. Halsey had been designated overall commander and would make the final decision of when to launch or scrub the mission, depending upon the situation, and Doolittle and his men would be under his command until launch.

Two days after the airmen had been informed of their mission, the Hornet's captain, Marc Mitscher, announced over the carrier's loudspeaker: "The target of this task force is Tokyo. The army is going to bomb Japan, and we're going to get them as close to the enemy as we can. This is a chance for all of us to give the Japs a dose of their own medicine." Cheers and screams of joy erupted throughout the ship, and sailors never missed an opportunity to congratulate or give a pat on the back to the airmen they passed in the halls. There had been a certain animosity between the army and navy personnel, a certain resentment at having these wrinkled, undisciplined army men aboard their ship and having to share sleeping quarters, showers, and galleys with them. After the announcement of their mission, navy personnel couldn't do enough for the airmen.

The risks of the mission were overwhelming; most described it as a "suicide mission." "Japan was so far away and so powerful and so well protected, the whole thing sounded impossible," mentioned one sailor. In his briefing to the men, Doolittle had told them about the risks—that even under the best circumstances and even with extra fuel tanks, the operation would be hard to pull off. Ideally, Hornet would get them within 450 miles of Japan. If discovered earlier, they could make it at 550, or with great luck at 650, they might make it past Japanese defenses and on to the Chinese landing fields. If discovery happened greater than 650 miles out, then the planes would try to take off and fly to Hawaii or Midway. Finally, if the task force was suddenly attacked, the B-25s would be pushed over the side so that fighter planes stored below on the hangar deck could be launched to protect the task force.

As all this information began to soak in and the airmen became aware of the extreme risk, the stress levels began to climb, and George Barr, like many others, found it difficult to sleep. During the long days at sea, the men had plenty of time to reflect on the odds of coming home. Maybe they weren't so fortunate, after all, to be going on this mission.

Battle Fatigue

At one of the final briefings, the men were told about the Japanese defenses that awaited them. Intelligence had determined that they would be greeted by over three hundred large-caliber antiaircraft guns and approximately five hundred fighter planes. From newsreels and classified reports coming back from China about Japanese atrocities, they were told that "if they were caught dropping bombs on Japan, the chances of their survival would be very, very slim." When one airman asked the navy briefer how captured flyers were normally treated, they were told that captives would be paraded through the streets, given some sort of kangaroo trial, and then publicly beheaded. This response sent a shiver through the group. George Barr, along with many of the others, would lie awake at night, thinking about the chances of a good outcome.

To avoid Japanese subs, the task force zigzagged across the Pacific. Then on April 18, with a storm gathering around them, the situation changed. It was approximately 7:50 AM, at a range of 690 miles from Japan, when the task force was spotted by enemy picket ships that quickly alerted Combined Headquarters in Tokyo. Admiral Yamamoto, commander of the Combined Fleet, ordered all ships and planes within a day's run of the reported enemy position to proceed there at once. The USS Enterprise intercepted this radio message and knew that, within hours, enemy carriers, cruisers, submarines, fighters, and bombers would be converging on the task force.

Admiral William "Bull" Halsey, the overall commander, faced a serious dilemma. He was still short of the launch range for Doolittle's bombers but could take them no farther, and the entire Japanese nation had been alerted and would be waiting to destroy the lightly armed task force. Halsey had long ago earned a reputation as a feisty, aggressive, risk-taking admiral; now those fine qualities would come into play. At 8:00 AM, Halsey flashed a message to CPT. Mitscher on the Hornet: "Launch Planes. To Col. Doolittle and gallant command: Good luck and God bless you."

Aboard the Hornet now, Klaxon horns bellowed, and all speakers announced: "Army pilots, man your planes." Most of the army crews were still getting dressed or waiting at tables in the mess area for stewards to bring their usual breakfast of powdered eggs, bacon, pancakes and coffee. The airmen thought it was just another drill; then they realized it was not only real, but their planes were about to be launched hundreds of miles short of where they had expected. One airman later said, "Upon hearing the announcement, cold chills ran up and down my back, and my knees became weak. I don't think there was a man leaving who really believed he would complete the mission in one piece."

Doolittle quickly called all the men together on the pitching deck and, as if to calm their feelings again, stated, "If there are any of you who don't want to go, just tell me. Because the chances of making it back are pretty slim." He then calmly ran through some coordinating instructions and finally said, "When we get to Chungking, I'm going to give you a party that you won't forget."

The following description illustrates the tremendous pressure these men were under in the last few frantic minutes before launch: Army and navy personnel rushed back and forth across the slanted, rain slick decks, topping off fuel tanks, arming bombs, and loading machine-gun ammunition. Finally, as a raging storm began to rise in its intensity, with thirty-foot waves and twenty-seven knot winds, the Hornet turned directly into the wind and pointed her bow straight for Tokyo Bay. With all crews now manning their planes, the time had come for takeoff, and only fifteen minutes had elapsed since the order to launch. Doolittle in the first plane inched his overloaded plane into position and waited for the flight deck officer's command to go. As Doolittle revved his engines, hearts were pounding, and all eyes were on the lead plane; they would now see if bombers could actually "fly off" a carrier at sea.

With sweaty hands and short breaths, Doolittle watched the flight officer's checkered flag shoot down to the deck as he yanked his feet from the brakes, and the plane began to shuffle down the short deck. As Doolittle went off the end of the flight deck seventy feet above the water, he momentarily disappeared from those on board. All present held their breath to see if plane number one had made it. Within seconds, the B-25 emerged from below the deck, struggling for altitude. A cheer went up from all aboard as Doolittle circled the ship. Years later, when someone asked Doolittle's navigator, Hank Potter, how he felt upon takeoff, he said, "We were particularly confident, since we had the best pilot in the air force flying us." Of those who lived through the mission, nearly all felt, at this point, that their chances of surviving the raid were close to zero.

George Barr was on the last plane to depart, "Bat Out of Hell," and bad luck seemed to follow the crew from the very start. The remainder of the crew consisted of pilot Lt. Bill Farrow from South Carolina, co-pilot Lt. Robert Hite from Texas, bombardier Cpl. Jacob Deshazer from Oregon, and engineer/gunner Sgt. Harold Spatz from Ohio. Because of a shortage of space on deck, this plane was parked with its tail hanging over the ship's stern. Then as the B-25s in front revved their engines, their prop blast caused Bat Out of Hell's nose to rise up and its tail to drop down over the side. Navy personnel were quick to throw a rope around the nose wheel to prevent the plane from slipping backward. In this effort to prevent the plane from slipping back, a sailor lost his footing and was swept into the left propeller, horribly chewing up one arm and spraying blood across the deck and over the plane's windshield. Gunner Deshazer, not yet aboard, helped move the injured sailor to a place of safety. The sailor survived, but his arm had to be amputated.

With all the other stress of preparing for takeoff, this incident of the sailor falling into their prop almost put the crew over the edge psychologically. As Cpl. DeShazer finally climbed into his position in the front of the plane and started strapping himself in, he noticed that the violent efforts to pull the plane's nose down had split the Plexiglas nose and left a jagged, foot-long crack, gaping open to the wind. DeShazer hesitated to mention the damage to the pilot, remembering the captain's order to push over the side any bomber that became disabled. So Bat Out of Hell took its place on the launch line and awaited the flagman's signal. The launch was successful, but immediately the crew felt air rushing through the cracked Plexiglas at 150 miles per hour, creating a dangerous drag that would use up more precious fuel.

The last plane was launched at 9:19 AM. It had taken a little over an hour to launch the sixteen bombers, and now they were strung out over a line aimed at Tokyo, 50 miles wide and 150 miles long. The first plane would reach Tokyo at around noon and then begin its bombing run. Those following would now be on their own and face their fate individually against an alarmed and waiting enemy.

Skimming low over the ocean at approximately fifty feet, the crews now had a chance to reflect upon their desperate situation. What would be waiting for them over the target? Where would they be when their fuel ran out? Would they ever see their families again? No one spoke unless he had to. Eventually, concerns began to focus on the navigator. With waning fuel tanks and overcast skies, were they on the right course? Would their fuel allow them to reach China? It was extremely difficult to get an exact reading on their position.

At approximately six hundred miles out, the formation flew under a Japanese flying boat that immediately radioed their position. The formation then flew over a Japanese cruiser, which also radioed their position to Tokyo. Then, at two hundred miles out, the weather cleared, and the ceiling and visibility were unlimited. Upon reaching Tokyo Bay, hundreds of ships there had a clear view of the raiders, and many radioed their position. So, there would be no surprise over the target. The entire Japanese Air Force would be waiting for them.

Ten B-25s were slated to hit the center of Tokyo, where most of the industry was concentrated; the other six were to hit steel mills, ammo dumps, aviation factories, shipyards; and fuel plants located along the flight paths. Now, as the bombers headed for their assigned areas, enemy fighters were spotted, but, strangely, most did not attack. Approaching their targets, pilots brought their planes up to 1200 feet, and bombardiers took over for the final run. As the bombs dropped away, the ships were two thousand to four thousand pounds lighter, easier to control, and much faster. A few of the planes could not find their targets and just picked anything that had a smokestack or looked like a factory. As the planes quickly rose for their bombing runs, antiaircraft guns found them, and enemy fighters would soon find them too. So they immediately dropped back down to treetop level to make their escape. One plane, upon being attacked by fighters over Tokyo Bay, quickly dropped its bombs into the bay, then gunned the engines to the max and was soon able to outrun the attackers. Plane 16, Bat Out of Hell, had been assigned the city of Nagoya. En route, several enemy fighters moved in behind them, but pilot Bill Farrow climbed into the clouds and lost them. "Bat" bombed an "oil tank farm" and an aircraft factory. Finally finishing the bomb run, Harold Spatz spotted eight Japanese fighters right on their tail. They were so close that he could see the flash of their guns as they started their attack. With its bomb load gone, "Bat" proved much faster than the attackers and soon outran them.

Their bombing runs complete, the sixteen bombers headed for the promised Chinese landing fields, passing over the island of Kyushu and then across the East China Sea. It was at this point that they received an unexpected gift. Just when most thought they'd have to ditch at sea, they encountered a 30 mile per hour tailwind that would give them an additional 250 miles of range—more than enough to reach the Chinese mainland.

"The Doolittle Raiders" had now been under unbelievable pressure for the past eight hours. They had manned their planes with nerves drawn tight and adrenaline flowing heavily, while surviving white-knuckle takeoffs and an 800-mile low-level flight, avoiding enemy fighters and antiaircraft fire. But, for many, their real ordeal was just beginning.

Unknown to the airmen, the U.S. military had tried unsuccessfully to arrange for airfields in Eastern China that would be controlled by friendly Chinese and stocked with aviation gas and oil. A radio directional beacon had also been shipped to the Far East to guide them in. But, due to the confusion and fog of war, none of these things that the planes so desperately needed for a safe landing were in place for the raiders as they approached the China coast.

Most planes had been in the air for over fifteen hours as they began arriving over the darkened, storm-covered coast of China. It's difficult to believe, in view of what these men had been through, that virtually all would report this phase of the mission as the most frightening.

As navigators like George Barr struggled with instruments to locate their positions, the planes, one by one, began to run out of fuel. It was at this point, in total darkness, being thrown around in a violent storm and not knowing if they were over water, land, or high mountains, that most crews faced the decision of riding the plane down and hoping to survive a crash landing or strapping on a parachutes and jumping into the black unknown of a storm and whatever lay below. Despite the fact that none of the airmen except Doolittle had ever used a parachute, nearly all chose to bail out.

Bill Birch, of plane number eleven, relates his experience in leaving the plane that his crew had become so attached to: "We wished each other luck, and then came the most fearsome event of my life: I jumped out of the plane into the night. The fact that we weren't absolutely certain as to what we were jumping into was a big worry. Would we land in the ocean, a river, lake, flat or mountainous terrain, or onto some Japanese soldier's bayonet?"

For most, landing in one piece just meant the beginning of another ordeal of survival. Much of the area of eastern China was controlled by the Japanese, and these new arrivals had just bombed their capital city and humiliated these ruthless warriors. The Japanese had been alerted and had been ordered to find and apprehend them at all costs.

Plane 16, Bat Out of Hell, arrived over the China coast with fuel to spare. With this extra fuel, they circled over the Chinese mainland for almost an hour, searching for the beacon that would lead them to the airfield mentioned by Doolittle in their briefing. Finally, pilot Bill Farrow decided to head straight west. At the same time, navigator George Barr suggested that they fly farther south to avoid the Japanese-held territories. Before this question could be resolved, the fuel warning light came on, and at that instant, there was a break in the clouds that allowed them to clearly see a city directly below. George Barr studied it momentarily and then announced that he was sure it was Nanchang, a Japanese-held city.

The engines began to cough as pilot Barrow clicked on the intercom and quickly announced that they were out of gas and ended with "we'll have to jump." They were flying at three thousand feet, and soon all five crew members had left the ship and were descending alone through the rainswept darkness. George Barr's worries about landing in enemy territory were turning out to be accurate. He landed in a rice paddy and, although on soft ground, he injured his right knee. Despite this handicap, he immediately started walking. Suddenly, he heard a loud shout and felt the cold muzzle of a rifle against his back. A group of soldiers surrounded him, searched him thoroughly, then tied his wrists in front and the crooks of his elbows from behind and took him to Nanchang.

Barr was taken to a headquarters building with a Japanese flag out front. Here he was led into a large room where, between ten and fifteen Japanese officers were seated around a large table. In the center of the table were bottles of whiskey, candy, and cigarettes. George was interrogated by one of the officers as the rest whispered among themselves. He refused to give anything beyond his name, rank, and serial number, although he did explain that he'd jumped from a plane and had hit his head upon landing and couldn't remember a thing.

Eventually, the questions ended, and he was taken to a different room and told to sleep. As he tried to sleep, he could only think about the previous twenty-four hours that had been so crammed with fear and emotion. He realized that his deadly ordeal was actually just beginning. Later in the day, the other crew-members of "Bat" were brought in by Japanese patrols, and their interrogations started.

Most know the attitude of the Japanese toward those who surrender or who are taken prisoner. But most are not aware of the American public's subtle, unstated opinion of those captured or those who surrendered. Even U.S. servicemen thought being captured was the worst thing that could happen to them. Barr recalled that, during his early training, everyone swore they'd rather die than be taken as a POW. He said that the underlying feeling by most of the flyers, but not all, was that those who were captured and failed to escape were losers, and when and if they ever got home, everyone would think they were failures. Barr later said, "Emotionally, it was the worst thing that had ever happened to me." As if to reinforce this feeling, the crew as a group was completely drained and felt helpless and no longer in control as they were placed in solitary confinement. Finally, as an ominous sign of what was to come, in nearby cells, crew members could hear fists or rifle butts slamming into flesh, followed by screaming and sobbing as they awaited more aggressive interrogation.

These interrogation techniques became more severe, and it was apparent that, somewhere, the Japanese had obtained a complete roster of those taking part in the raid and even the name of the aircraft carrier that brought them into Japanese waters. So, those asking the questions already knew the answers, and when an airman gave a false or deceptive response, guards reacted violently. They could not expect things to get any better. It had been drilled into them, the attitude of the Japanese toward those who surrendered or allowed themselves to be captured. This attitude was not just a personal thing with the Japanese; it had been institutionalized in a Japanese army manual that was issued to all recruits. The manual has this to say about capture: "Bear in mind the fact that to be captured means not only that you disgrace yourself, but your parents and family will never be able to hold their heads up again. Always save the last bullet for yourself." The Japanese officer's manual stated it even more directly: "Any commander who allows his unit to surrender to the enemy without fighting to the last man, shall be punished by death."

Out of the eighty men and sixteen planes that took part in the raid, only eight airmen had been unfortunate enough to be captured by the Japanese. Five of these were from the crew of "Bat Out of Hell," and three were from "The Green Hornet." The brutality that these men endured was worse than cattle being prepared for slaughter. Every night, they were taken individually for questioning, usually by a different set of interrogators using ever more frightful tactics. The threat of death by decapitation was regularly mentioned. Then, suddenly without any prior notice, the prisoners were blindfolded, handcuffed, leg cuffed, and placed aboard a plane and taken to Shanghai. From there, they were put on another long plane ride to Tokyo and finally turned over to the Japanese military police, who were similar to the KGB or Gestapo. These men were experts in the ancient art of torture, and they seldom failed to obtain a complete confession from their captives.

In Tokyo, the men were housed together, but the interrogations and beatings continued. They hadn't bathed, shaved, or changed clothes since their capture, and the food ration remained three cups of tea and six pieces of stale bread each day. This inhumane treatment and their awareness that the Japanese had killed millions of Chinese men, women, and children, caused the prisoners to give up all hope of surviving. They became resigned to the fact that they would eventually be killed, and they figured it was now just a matter of when and how.

This hopeless attitude caused them to decide as a group that, since the Japanese knew every detail of the raid, it really didn't matter any longer if they signed confessions, even those written in Japanese and just maybe, the beatings would stop. The confessions were based upon bits and pieces of information that was beaten out of the airmen, plus propaganda that had been written or broadcast about the raid. Their interrogators had woven into the confessions, references to the act of bombing civilian homes and schools and killing innocent women and children.

Their interrogations complete, the eight men were again bound hand and foot and on June 15, 1942, were moved by train to Nagasaki. Traveling in an open railcar, the soot from the train engine added to their wild-animal look. From Nagasaki, they were placed aboard a freighter to Shanghai. When they reached Shanghai, they were housed in an old hotel, which had been converted into a prison. In one of the ballrooms, the guards had constructed a bamboo cage that was approximately 20'×10'×7' and was raised two feet above the floor. Inside this cage were approximately thirty Chinese, including two women. A tub in one corner with a board over it served as the toilet. Two Chinese died the first night, and their bodies were not removed for three days. During the next four months, the men would live in this "hell hole" and be starved, dehydrated, and refused medical attention while their minds, bodies, and spirits steadily deteriorated.

Without explanation, the guards arrived one day and took the airmen to one of the rooms in a hotel that had a bathroom with running water and ordered them to bathe. Soon after getting cleaned up, the eight captive airmen were moved to a military prison just outside of Shanghai and, for the first time, they each had their own cell, a 9'×5' concrete box. At no time during their captivity were they able to receive Red Cross assistance or send or receive mail.

Soon, a trial began for the flyers, and each day they were taken to the Thirteenth Army Military Court to answer for their "war crimes."

In the courtroom, three Japanese judges sat high above them, as the airmen under heavy guard were forced to stand below. All listened as a military prosecutor droned on for hours in Japanese. No interpreter was provided, and the flyers were not allowed to present a defense. The confessions that were beaten out of the men were now introduced as evidence and examined very carefully by the prosecutor. Three of the flyers had mentioned in their confessions that just before releasing their bombs, they had seen a school or schoolyard, and one gunner, Harold Spatz, even mentioned firing his machine gun into the schoolyard. This school had allegedly been destroyed by the raiders, and several children had been killed or injured. It was later speculated that Japanese antiaircraft fire had fallen on the school and caused the damage.

The prosecutor seemed to focus his attention on these three airmen and their confessions about the school. This, despite the fact that the confessions were beaten out of the men and that they were forced to sign a statement they couldn't read. There was also no way of knowing if the guards had made up the details of the confession or if interrogators had asked leading questions. The men were barely coherent as they were brought into the courtroom each day. The pilot of plane 6, Dean Hallmark, had to be carried into the courtroom, and George Barr fainted and lay unconscious during most of the proceedings. Because of his red hair, Barr had suffered horribly at the hands of his guards. They thought he looked like a monkey and were always taunting him with sticks or clubs.

The "War Crimes Trial" was over in less than three days, and the results or sentences were announced in Japanese. When the airmen asked the interpreter to explain, he stated, "They asked me not to tell you." The results of the trial were sent to Tokyo for Prime Minister Tojo and Army Chief of Staff Sugiyama to review and then to provide a recommendation to the emperor for his final decision. Sugiyama wanted all the raiders executed as an example to others who might be planning to bomb Japan. Tojo urged leniency toward the raiders, except he agreed that those guilty of killing innocent civilians should be executed. The emperor agreed with Tojo, and word was sent to the chief prosecutor that all sentences should be commuted to life in prison except for three of the flyers. On October 14, 1942, Lt. Dean

Hallmark, Lt. William Farrow, and Sgt. Harold Spatz were informed that they had been found guilty by the War Crimes Court and were sentenced to be executed by firing squad. The executions were then scheduled for the next day, and the men were allowed to write one letter home that would be delivered by the Red Cross.

The horror of this brutal process taking place before him was more than George Barr could endure. At several points along the way from April to October, George just could not imagine how things could get any worse, and yet at every turn, they became dramatically worse. It was at this point that the trauma became too much for George and he began to lose touch with reality.

After the executions, the five remaining airmen were kept in solitary confinement at a military prison just outside of Shanghai. Their cells were unheated, and the winter of 1942 was one of the coldest on record. There was a freeze that never lifted, and although the men were given extra clothing, they still suffered tremendously from the bone-chilling cold. Alone in their cells, suffering from dysentery and beriberi, the men were now in advanced stages of vitamin and mineral deficiencies, and each began to experience extreme neurological or mental disorders. They couldn't concentrate or sustain a thought, and the slightest irritation caused a major outburst. All developed pains and sores over their entire bodies.

On the one-year anniversary of their raid, the five captives were roped, blindfolded, cuffed, and chained together as they were flown to Nanking. Here, at a newly built prison, they were once again placed in solitary confinement, but this time the cells were made of wood, and eventually each airman was given a table and chair. Food was still only a bowl of rice each day, which was not enough to sustain life, and the men continued their long slide into starvation. Finally, on December 1, 1943, Lt. Meder, co-pilot of plane number 6 died. He had been starved to death. Now a heavier veil of depression descended on the group, as each of the men became more aware that they could die tomorrow and no one would ever know what had happened to them.

As conditions in the new prison continued to get worse, Bob Hite, co-pilot of plane 16, wrote a letter of complaint to the prison governor.

In this letter, Hite complained that their treatment was against the Geneva Convention and that their food rations were outrageous and inadequate. He closed the letter with this final plea: "If you can't do anything useful, please give us the Holy Bible to read."

Within a few days of turning in this letter, the prison captain paid them a visit. He asked them what they wanted to eat. The prisoners told him they only wanted what they would get from any army mess: chicken, steak, eggs, milk, vegetables, and chocolate. The next day, their food improved. They received soup or rice three times a day with pieces of bread. In addition, they were allowed to read books written in English, including the Bible.

The winter of 1944–1945 was the worst in over one hundred years, and it brought unimagined suffering to George Barr and his fellow captives. The end of November brought heavy snows that coated everything until March. The compound was unheated and, to supplement their ragged prison pajamas, guards issued extra clothing, but the prisoners had to continue wearing their Japanese slippers. Under these conditions, the only way they could get warm was to run outside, but their slippers kept coming off. Ignoring the cold, the men removed their slippers and ran barefoot. Prior to returning to their cells, the guards ordered them not to use drinking water to clean the mud from their feet but to use snow instead. George Barr refused and began using drinking water to wash his feet. Seeing this, a guard shoved George Barr toward his cell, and George reacted violently by elbowing the man in the stomach. The guard did not let this incident go unpunished, and, after putting the other Americans in their cells, ten guards gathered around George and beat and kicked him until he fell to the ground unconscious. He was then tightly strapped into a straitjacket that was much too small for him, causing extreme pain that made him scream for hours. Being bound up like this for hours on the verge of suffocation caused George Barr to mentally start to come apart. After approximately twelve hours, the jacket was removed, but George was so incoherent, he thought for days that he was still wearing it.

In June of 1945, as the war was coming to an end, the prisoners were once again hooded, handcuffed, and moved by train to a military prison near Peiping (Beijing). There, they were placed in solitary confinement.

Battle Fatigue

The guards at this prison were severe and worked "by the book." In their cells, the prisoners were made to sit on a bench facing the wall ten hours a day. George Barr's pale, freckled complexion and red hair again caused the guards to "single him out" for more brutal treatment. George spent most of his days in Peiping unconscious, too weak to stand or even eat solid food. His mental condition had deteriorated to the point where, when his food was delivered to him, he lay in a stupor, unable to understand what to do with it.

On August 9th, a B-29 bomber dropped an atomic bomb on the city of Nagasaki, and the next day, Japanese leaders announced that they would accept America's terms for surrender. Then, on August 20, 1945, guards unlocked George Barr's cell door and took him to an area used by the guards, where they allowed him to bathe and shave. Then dressed him in the uniform he'd been wearing when he was captured. George was too weak to do much for himself, so the guards assisted. Then he, along with the other three Doolittle airmen, were taken before a prison captain to hear this announcement: "The war is over. You can go home now."

In his mental condition, George could not understand what was happening. For several days after his liberation, he believed he was dead. He justified this by the fact that he had been reunited with his fellow airmen, and they were all happy and smiling. So, in his mind, they were all dead and had been reunited in heaven. A Red Cross truck arrived at the prison to take George and his fellow prisoners to the Grand Hotel in the center of Peiping. Along the way, streets were filled with cheering crowds and many heavily armed Chinese in uniform. George had just spent over three years in solitary confinement, and his brain couldn't process the scene around him. At the hotel, he was swept up in the crowd of celebrating allies. But everything was happening so fast he couldn't keep up with it. As it became apparent that something was wrong with George Barr, a senior American officer staying at the hotel had him carried to his room, and a doctor summoned. George was given a blood transfusion and medication to help him sleep. The next morning, his fear and paranoia were as strong as ever, and he thought the hotel, food, and nurse were all part of a Japanese trick to confuse him. He thought at any moment it would all be taken away, and he would be handcuffed and sent back to solitary confinement.

After several days of rest and good food, the local military doctor gave approval for everyone but George to fly on to Chungking to begin the long journey home. Before leaving, the three men who had been together for so long dropped by Barr's room to say good-bye. George was totally confused. He didn't understand why they were going home, and he was still in captivity. The next morning when he woke up, he couldn't remember anything that had happened during the past few days, not even his release from prison.

It was another week before George Barr could walk using a cane, but his mind was still not healing properly. The flurry of activity and sudden consumption of rich foods and drink apparently caused his mental disorders to return in full force. The old suspicions and paranoia overwhelmed him to the point where every Asian person he saw looked Japanese, and he imagined that Caucasians were working for the Japanese; even when looking out the window, all his mind could see were Japanese. Although the medical staff and other GIs would assure him that he was free now and no longer had to worry about his safety, they still wouldn't let him go home.

During this period of recovery, he couldn't sleep, and when he did, he would wake up screaming from nightmares of being beaten by guards, bound up in a straitjacket, or subjected to the water torture and not being able to breathe.

On September 12, 1945, George was flown to Kunming and placed in a bare room. He refused to allow any more transfusions or for nurses to take his temperature. He thought they were trying to take over his brain. Finally, he did accept some vitamins and mild sleeping pills. This same night, the nightmares returned and were so violent that he fell out of bed and raged uncontrollably. Security was called, and for his own safety, George was physically restrained by three orderlies and transferred to the psychiatric ward of the hospital where, as his paranoia had imagined all along, he awoke alone in a room with padded walls and barred windows. It all added up to him—he was still a prisoner of the Japanese and back in solitary confinement.

Battle Fatigue

George Barr's condition was not improving and, as time passed, nurses and doctors changed, and his records were lost. When he tried to tell the hospital staff that he was one of the famed "Doolittle Raiders," they thought he was suffering from delusions. But one psychiatric doctor believed him, and when George told the doctor he was being held captive by the Japanese, the doctor did everything to convince him he was not. The bars from his windows were removed, and George was allowed to leave his room and visit with other patients in the dayroom.

This breakthrough lasted only a few days, and then George reverted back to his extreme paranoia. He demanded that the nurses kill him with an overdose of medication or lethal injection, anything, just to end his mental suffering. With this latest outburst, hospital officials decided that George would need extensive hospitalization.

The type of treatment George required was not available in China, so on October 9, 1945, he and an orderly were sent to the airport to begin the long journey back to the United States. As he and the orderly walked to the plane, George, still thinking he was a prisoner of the Japanese, saw a chance to escape and started running toward the perimeter fence. Then, suddenly something snapped, and he fell to the ground unconscious. When he regained consciousness, he was in a straitjacket and tied to a stretcher aboard a plane flying west over a high mountain range.

The plane finally landed in Calcutta, and George was placed in a hospital ward with several other wounded veterans. That night, his mind was terrorized again by the horrors of his long confinement, and his violent screaming terrified the nurses. They moved George to a padded room to protect him from himself.

After a few days in Calcutta, George and his orderly continued on to San Francisco. When they landed, his orderly turned over custody of George to the local field hospital and disappeared. George had arrived with no baggage, no records, no identification, and no money. When doctors attempted to interview him about his last assignment, he told them an unbelievable story of having been part of the Doolittle raid on Tokyo, and the doctors just shook their heads. Following this interview by the doctors, George was given a pair of pajamas and led to a room where he sat down on the bed and began to look around. On a nearby table was a small penknife. Exhausted and depressed from his long trip and believing he was somehow still a prisoner of the Japanese, George saw this as a perfect opportunity to end it all. He grabbed the penknife and with all his strength, drove it into his chest. Then he waited. Nothing happened; he didn't even bleed. Determined to finish the job, he grabbed a nearby lamp, ripped the electrical cord out, and, with one end, he fashioned a noose around his neck, stepped up on a chair, and tied the other end around the ceiling light fixture, then jumped. The light fixture pulled from the ceiling with a loud explosion, and George landed unhurt in the middle of the floor. This commotion brought the medical officer and two orderlies running. They dragged George away to a locked padded cell with bars on the window and a slit in the door. At this point, George began screaming that he only wanted to die—wouldn't they please just let him die?

During World War II, army regulations called for wounded servicemen who required long-term care to be sent to the military hospital closest to their home. In this effort, army officials mistakenly sent George to Iowa rather than New York. The reason for this confusion was that the army had chosen the location where George had entered military service, rather than New York, where he had been born and raised. George had attended Northland College in Wisconsin so he could take part in the Flying Cadets program, and this is where he joined the military. The closest army hospital was located at Clinton, Iowa, and that's where George was sent.

On October 19, 1945, George and five other seriously ill patients were secured in straitjackets and carried aboard a special train heading east. The slow train carried him through one small town after another, and at night he was forced to sleep under a restraining sheet until they finally reached Clinton, Iowa, where he was locked up in a ward with seven extremely disturbed soldiers. In George's damaged mind, he was still a prisoner of the Japanese, and all efforts to convince him he was free were just seen as further tricks or torture directed by his captors.

As the weeks began to pass, it became apparent that George Barr had become lost in the system and would never be reunited with his family.

But that was about to change. From an early age, George's life had been a struggle. He had been orphaned at six months of age when his father drowned in a boating accident. Then a short time later, when his mother could not support him and an older sister, they were sent to live in a foster home in Yonkers, New York. As a teenager, he and his sister were taken into the home of a local social worker, Mrs. Charles A. Towns. She and her husband were determined to provide a strong family environment for the two children and instill in them a proper sense of values. After the children left home, Mrs. Towns stayed in close contact with them. She had followed George's career in the air corps and had been notified of his capture after the Tokyo raid. When the Pacific war ended, someone had sent a two-lined message to Mr. and Mrs. Towns, stating that George had been released by the Japanese, and he would be coming home soon. This was all they received, and as the weeks passed with no further word from George, Mrs. Towns began writing letters and making phone calls for help in locating "her son." Finally, she contacted Gen. Doolittle and asked for his help. The general called the army personnel center in Washington, and they were soon able to tell him that Second Lt. George Barr was a patient at Schick Army General Hospital in Clinton, Iowa.

George's sister was pregnant at the time but sent her husband Bill to see George. He was still very ill, and his old suspicions and doubts persisted, and he drew back and refused to recognize or communicate with his brother-in-law. Mrs. Towns soon came to visit, with the same result. It was at this point that Mrs. Towns contacted the general again and told him of the family's concern for George. General Doolittle quickly agreed to go visit George and see what he could do. The following is a summary of Gen. Doolittle's visit in his own words:

"I immediately flew out to Clinton, Iowa, where the Army sleuths had located him. Not knowing George's true condition, I had to be cautious, because I knew he would be surprised to see me. I greeted him like an old friend, and George immediately broke into tears. I was the first military person he had seen that he knew since his buddies had left him in China. He seemed very normal to me, so we went for a walk, and he tried to tell me everything he could. He was hesitant at first, but then the tears flowed, and the words began to pour out.

Catharsis was obviously what he needed. I was shocked and found it difficult to believe that he had not seen a doctor and had no money, no clothes, and no military status, except that of "patient." The last of my Tokyo Raiders to come home needed help, and I was going to see that he got it.

"I can say unreservedly that I have never been so angry in my life as I was when George told me what had happened to him. I walked with him back to the ward and went immediately to see the hospital commander, where I unloaded Doolittle's worst verbal fury on his head. I won't repeat what I said, because it would burn a hole in this page. I will say that George was quickly outfitted in a new uniform, complete with the ribbons he didn't know he had earned and was given a check for over $7,000 in back pay and orders promoting him to first lieutenant. Best of all, he was seen immediately by a psychiatrist and began the slow road back to recovery.

"Before I left, I asked George if he remembered that, before we left the Hornet, I had promised the fellows a party in Chungking. He said, 'Yes, sir, I do.'

"'Well, George, we never had that party because you and the rest of the fellows couldn't make it. But I'm going to keep that promise. The whole gang is invited to be my guests in Miami on my birthday on December 14. I want you to come. I'll send an airplane for you.'

"My visit, George told me years later, was a turning point in his recovery."

George Barr did attend the general's birthday party and was the center of attention, with an outpouring of affection and concern for his welfare by all those in attendance. It would take a little over two years for George Barr's full recovery to take place. But soon after Gen. Doolittle's visit, he was transferred to Mitchell Field on Long Island, New York, to be near his family. Then, with the help of Lt. Bob Hite, his co-pilot on "Bat Out of Hell," who was stationed nearby, George began to make rapid progress. Around the middle of 1946, George was returned to light duty and quickly promoted to captain. That same year, he fell in love with a lovely young lady, and they were soon married.

Because it is an inspiring story of success in overcoming about as severe a case of Battle Fatigue as one might encounter, I've devoted considerable space to the service, injury, and recovery of George Barr. No one who has ever suffered or is suffering from this condition can read George's story and not feel a connection with him and his agonizing struggle to recover. The story also provides insight for veterans, their families, and health care workers as to some of the simple acts, conditions, or procedures that have succeeded in putting lives back together and promoting the healing process.

An important point that might be over-looked is the role the active military played in being part of the rehabilitation process. The intervention of a general officer to keep soldiers on active duty during their healing process should not be necessary, as it was with George Barr. But, unfortunately, the policy of the active forces is to transfer responsibility for rehabilitation to the VA or the family just as quickly as they can. This, despite the healing benefits that might be gained from staying on active duty, even in some limited way.

Finally, no matter how serious an individual's psychological injury or mental condition might be, this story gives one hope that it is possible to eventually return to a "normal" life. (The above story was inspired by the book *The First Heroes: The Extraordinary Story of the Doolittle Raid—America's First World War II Victory*, by Craig Nelson, 2002).

Chapter Four

Diagnosis and Treatment

Battle Fatigue is little discussed and virtually shunned as a subject for combat training, because its symptoms are a contradiction of the normal positive qualities and traits that the military system attempts to rigidly instill in our fighting men and women. Within the environment of a military training center, instructors strive to develop strong, positive qualities such as physical strength, courage, perseverance, and mental endurance. Battle Fatigue, on the other hand, represents just the opposite, or rather a breakdown of these positive traits, and becomes something that soldiers avoid at all costs, rather than risk being unable to perform their jobs and severely criticized for displaying the symptoms of weakness. That being said, even strong "John Wayne" type warriors who inspire us with their courage and bravery can often become Battle Fatigue casualties if left in intense combat too long.

The seriousness of this type of injury to mission accomplishment was made apparent in 1945, as U.S. Marines approached the Japanese home islands for the battle of Iwo Jima, where they encountered some of the fiercest fighting of the war. This ten-square mile slaughterhouse produced twenty-seven Medals of Honor, more than any other battle in the history of the United States.

In May of 2000, Bantam Books published *Flags of Our Fathers*, written by James Bradley, which was later made into a movie directed by Clint Eastwood. The story is about the lives of the six marines who raised the American flag over Iwo Jima during that historic battle. The six were typically young, red-blooded Americans who had enlisted or were drafted into the service following Pearl Harbor. Through glimpses of their training and while aboard ship en route to Iwo Jima, we were shown just how normal and "All-American" the six Marines were. Then, the actual invasion was shown, with men charging out of landing crafts into the muzzles of Japanese machine guns and heavy artillery. Blood and gore were everywhere, as the enemy took their heavy toll of the young Americans. Each Japanese soldier had been ordered to kill ten Americans before they were themselves killed or before they committed *hari-kari* (suicide).

The six Marines, like all the others who landed on the island, were exposed to the most extreme and vicious combat in the annals of warfare. The barbaric Japanese soldiers were determined to die for the emperor. But first they wanted to kill and mutilate as many invaders as possible, using any and all tricks and deceptions, such as pretending to surrender, then killing their would-be captors as they came forward, or pretending to be wounded and in perfect English, calling out for a medic. Then, as a navy corpsman would rush in to help, the Japanese soldier would explode a grenade, killing both individuals. This extreme and prolonged combat produced the symptoms of Battle Fatigue in virtually all those who participated.

The six flag raisers were a small group of Marines (actually five marines and one navy corpsman) who had come together just as the key terrain feature on the island, Mount Suribachi, fell to the Americans. This little group had been given the assignment to climb to the top of the mountain and raise the American flag in order to inspire their fellow Marines.

What made the event extraordinary was the presence of Associated Press photographer, Joe Rosenthal.

As the Marines hoisted the American flag on an old piece of rusty pipe, their image was caught on film by Rosenthal. This picture would become the most recognized and reproduced of all time and would become a symbol to the nation of courage, heroism, and the highest ideals of what the country was fighting for. It did something else; it gave instant fame and immortality to the six men involved. By the time the war department realized the significance of the photograph and the celebrity status of the six Marines, three had been killed in action, and another wounded. The three remaining Marines were quickly taken out of action and returned home as heroes, to raise money for the war effort in an unprecedented War Bond crusade.

Upon their arrival home, the 3 surviving flag raisers, one still in bandages, were invited to the White House where President Harry Truman kicked off the largest bond drive of the war. The three men were expected to tour the country, talk about their war experiences and promote the sale of bonds.

The story follows the men on this "Bond Tour" and examines their lives as they struggle with the horrors and nightmares of savage combat. Nowhere in the story does the military ever recognize that the men have a problem or offer any sort of treatment. They are on their own to try to calm the demons that torment them. Two turn to alcohol to dull the images and to provide an escape. Eventually, after much substance abuse, one of the Marines, an American Indian, is found lying face down in a cornfield on an Indian reservation, dead from cold and exposure after a night of heavy drinking.

Only one of the three, the father of the author, John Bradley, was able to return home and have what appeared to be a normal life. He married his childhood sweetheart, owned and operated a funeral home, had eight children, and joined all the right civic clubs. He was able to do this by putting his war experiences behind him and never mentioning it or the flag-raising incident to anyone, not even his family. His medals, newspaper clippings, uniforms, and dog tags were put in a box and hidden deep in a backroom closet. From all outward appearances, John Bradley had succeeded in escaping the demons that pursued him, but upon closer examination, the story reveals that he had not,—they were just well hidden from all those around him. In interviews with his wife, it was revealed that she often awoke to find her husband crying in his sleep or calling the names of his fallen comrades.

Before coming ashore at Iwo Jima, everyone in Bradley's company had been matched up with a buddy to watch out for them as further insurance that no one would be alone on the deadly beach. Bradley had been matched up with Ralph Ignatowski, nicknamed Iggy. Due to his duties as a medic, Bradley was all over the battlefield with no opportunity to look out for Iggy. At some point during the opening battle Iggy strayed to the edge of the action and was captured by the Japanese. Two days later as caves were being cleared of dead Japanese, Iggy's body was discovered. Bradley, who was nearby, was called over to examine it. Nothing he had seen in the viciousness of the recent fighting, nor the sadistic brutality of the Japanese could prepare him for what he was about to see. The enemy had tortured and horrible mutilated Iggy's body, which had been partially skinned, eyes gouged out, nose, ears and genitals hacked off and his torso stabbed repeatedly with bayonets. As Iggy's buddy, the one who was supposed to watch out for him, Bradley felt responsible for what had happened. For the remainder of his long life, he would be haunted by feelings of guilt and by nightmares of Iggy's grotesque corpse. Then almost fifty years after the battle, John Bradley suffered a serious heart attack and, as he lay near death, began calling out to his Marine buddy who didn't make it off the island.

With the perspective of hindsight, it's now easy to see that every Marine who participated in the battle for Iwo Jima suffered some level of Battle Fatigue. The tragedy is that John Bradley was not recognized at the time to be suffering from Battle Fatigue and that no treatment was provided to him by the Marine Corps or Veterans Administration.

Close to ten thousand of the seventy thousand Marines who fought on Iwo Jima were labeled as extreme Battle Fatigue cases and evacuated from the island, physically unable to continue the fight. With these high numbers from this one battle alone, the military should have become experts at planning for, identifying, and treating the condition. But sadly, they have not, and with each succeeding war, the military is relearning the same lessons all over again and suffering the same unnecessary casualties.

As the final numbers were tallied, it was determined that, because of the prolonged exposure to the savage violence and uncontrolled death and destruction on this tiny island, some units suffered losses of over 80 percent, and fully one-third of the twenty-seven thousand casualties were labeled Battle Fatigue. More recently, over 250,000 Vietnam combat veterans, over thirty years after the end of that war, meet the Veterans Administration criteria for Battle Fatigue or PTSD. In the case of our current wars in the Middle East with its multiple tours, estimates range as high as 60 percent of our servicemen and servicewomen returning with some level of psychological injury.

Although Battle Fatigue is a well-known condition in the medical community and has been around since man's first efforts at organized combat, there has been little effort by modern military commanders to understand or appreciate its affects on individual soldiers and their units. Commanders continue to see it as an issue for doctors to deal with, and most still look at this injury as a sign of weakness or even cowardice or possibly a cover for malingering, to avoid being sent back to the front lines. Sadly, as Gen. Patton discovered in 1943, the injury is real, and any person or unit subjected to Battle Fatigue will have their fighting capacity greatly reduced.

Every year, thousands of our young men and women enter the military primarily for educational benefits, and as the military begins to train these eager recruits, they soon learn that they are being trained "to close with and kill or capture the enemy." Then, at the completion of their training, many are routinely sent off on "peacekeeping" missions or, as in the case of Afghanistan and Iraq, to a shooting war. This entire process is done with little regard for potential psychological injuries. Then, at the end of their term of service, these young men and women are discharged and returned to civilian life, where most make the transition without difficulty and go on to enjoy normal, productive lives. However, some, because of the intense combat they have endured, have difficulty adjusting. Others, because of a delicate emotional makeup, are slow to adjust to a normal routine and probably should never have been brought into the armed forces to begin with.

Many generations ago, our armed forces instituted a system of basic military training to, among other things, "weed out" those who were physically or mentally incapable of facing the rigors of combat. This program was generally effective in insuring that all newly minted soldiers and sailors had the basic skills and stamina needed to survive on the battlefield. However, today, as our voluntary military, which is deeply committed around the world, struggles to meet its recruiting goals, those in the basic training business are encouraged and, in some cases, directed to graduate every soldier, sailor, or airman who enters, regardless of physical or emotional difficulties, in order to make their quotas.

On May 1, 2007, a Pentagon panel of senior medical officers released its preliminary findings, which revealed that the military is putting already strained troops at greater risk of mental health problems because of repeated deployments to Iraq and Afghanistan. The report was considered an urgent warning of an overburdened health care system. The panel chairman, army surgeon Gen. Donald Arthur said, "More than one third of troops and veterans currently suffer from problems such as traumatic brain injury and post-traumatic stress disorder."

With a prolonged Middle East war, those numbers are expected to worsen, and current staffing and money for military health care won't be able to meet this need, the group said in its report. "The system of care for psychological health that has evolved in recent decades is not sufficient to meet the needs of today's forces and their beneficiaries and will not be sufficient to meet the needs in the future," the fourteen-member group said.

The panel was very harsh in its criticism of Pentagon policies it considered overly conservative and out-of-date. The group called for more money and a fundamental shift in treatment to focus on prevention and screening, rather than simply relying on soldiers to come forward on their own. They cited the well-known stigma that most soldiers believe they will encounter and the ridicule and damage that will be caused to their careers if they acknowledge having psychological problems. The four-page report comes amid attention to troop and veterans' care following recent disclosures of shoddy outpatient treatment at Walter Reed Army Medical Center. The panel found that 38 percent of army personnel and 31 percent of Marines reported psychological concerns such as traumatic brain injury and post-traumatic stress disorders after returning from deployment. The statistics for the National Guard were much higher, 49 percent, with numbers expected to grow even more because of repeated deployments and the additional strains of a civilian job and community that are left behind.

A related issue that shows the damage repeated deployments can have on our military is in the category of desertions, which often occur as a result of psychological stress or injury. Throughout history, one of the most serious crimes a soldier could commit was to desert his post. If he chose to desert in the face of the enemy, the result was often death by firing squad. This punishment provided a strong incentive for soldiers to face the enemy regardless of their mental or physical health. Today, that punishment is rare, and the circumstances are usually not as dire. The modern military considers a soldier to be a deserter if he or she has been absent from a unit without permission for over thirty days. Senior military leaders often gauge a unit's morale and quality of leadership by its desertion rate. A close examination of the desertion rates for army combat units fighting in Iraq shows a steady increase of almost 85 percent from 2003 to 2008. Army officials who have attempted to determine the reasons for these higher numbers have found that the single most important factor in an individual's decision to desert is the number of repeat assignments to the Middle East. This situation is in contrast to the navy, whose desertion numbers actually went down during the same time period and the Marine Corps, whose numbers have remained virtually unchanged throughout five years of war.

While the total numbers for the army are still lower than those experienced during the Vietnam War when the draft was in effect, the steady increase is a cause for concern.

A recent article in the *Wall Street Journal* concerning the military's efforts to meet recruiting goals indicates that corners are being cut. For example, the age limit for basic trainees has been raised to forty-two. To gain a larger pool of recruits, aptitude scores for admission have been reduced to less than thirty points out of a possible one hundred, and more recruits with police records and medical problems are being accepted.

The lowering of recruiting standards is significant, because past experience has shown that those who enter service with at least a high school diploma, score well on the aptitude test, require no moral waivers, and perform very well under the rigors of combat. Those who fail to meet the requirements and who must have the rules bent for them, often become problems, both on active duty and later for the Veterans Administration. However, once accepted and trained, the health and welfare of these individuals becomes the responsibility of the nation. This shortsighted practice, then, is setting up the conditions, particularly in the combat branches, for future Battle Fatigue casualties.

During recent years, as our soldiers have returned from Iraq and Afghanistan, we've come to realize that the destruction of an individual's or a unit's fighting capacity from Battle Fatigue is not the only loss. Veterans' hospitals all across America have a growing population of these very real casualties of both recent and past conflicts. Although now more politely labeled "post-traumatic stress disorder," or PTSD, this is more than just a simple psychological injury, this condition will permanently damages lives. This is not a phantom illness.

Medical research conducted after three recent wars has shown the comprehensive effects of this disorder on families, children, employment, and particularly on the veteran, all of which is a tremendous loss to the nation.

Once released from active duty, this small population of psychologically injured veterans often has difficulty re-entering civilian life. Some are tormented by their experiences and can't sleep. The next step for some is to self-medicate by taking a couple of drinks of alcohol before bedtime to get through the terrors of the night. For other veterans, crowds or interaction with people causes unbearable anxiety. Many of these veterans quit their jobs and find relief by living alone in isolated or remote locations. Then, since these isolated veterans have no income, many wind up homeless and adrift. Let me say again that the vast majority of discharged veterans make the transition to civilian life with few difficulties and go on to enjoy normal and productive lives. Our focus, however, is on the small group of veterans who account for a disproportionate share of society's ills and can be traced back to this growing population that suffers from serious Battle Fatigue. Recent medical research has shown that significant numbers of the homeless, alcoholics, drug users, the perpetrators of domestic violence, and the unemployed are, in fact, veterans who have been diagnosed with serious Battle Fatigue.

Wives and other family members are in a good position to detect the signs and symptoms of Battle Fatigue. The following is an example of how one caring wife was able to get her soldier husband the treatment he needed:

"Knowledge is empowering," said Kathy, an army wife of more than ten years. When her husband returned from Iraq fourteen months ago, she began working to find ways to help him.

"He was in trouble pretty soon after he came back, which meant we were in trouble," she said. "He had terrible insomnia, nightmares, rages, and days of complete withdrawal. I knew enough to know that he probably had PTSD, but he wasn't diagnosed by a doctor and wouldn't go to a therapist. I figured, 'Well, what do I not know that would help me help him?'"

Kathy began doing research, visiting the library, reading articles in medical journals, and searching the Internet. Every now and then she would run across commentaries and medical briefs that indicated a link between PTSD and physical problems. She printed out a few stories and spoke to her husband about them. "All I did was say 'look, you could face serious health issues or wind up, down the road, being really sick, and I want you healthy.'"

Kathy got her husband to a regular doctor for a physical. The medical exam led to a lengthy discussion with the physician, which led to her husband agreeing to counseling.

"I don't think he'd be receiving help today if I hadn't found a back door to get him through. He wouldn't go for counseling because he couldn't face the idea that he was suffering from anything resembling a mental problem. So I had to start with something he could face" (Ledford 2008).

At the end of 2007, a panel of Pentagon military doctors was asked to study the effects of mental health issues on unit readiness, with particular emphasis on repeated deployments. Aside from those who suffered from traumatic brain injury and injuries associated with direct combat, the panel's final report revealed that a high percentage of soldiers were suffering from anxiety and extreme stress as a result of multiple combat tours. These symptoms eventually revealed themselves in PTSD. People can draw their own conclusions about the readiness of units deploying with a high percentage of personnel suffering from psychological injuries.

The report also stated the well-known fact that the military health care system is being overwhelmed by the large numbers of casualties produced by the wars in Iraq and Afghanistan. This revealed for the first time that current assets are not sufficient to handle the increased load of psychological injuries. The fix, as described by the panel, was, predictably, more money devoted to this area of care and the need to initiate a Defense Department program of prevention for psychological injuries, often referred to as "unseen injuries."

This past year, Congress authorized 150 million dollars to the VA to determine the effectiveness of early intervention. Returning soldiers from the battlefields in the Middle East were routinely screened and surveyed thirty days after arriving home and some approximately six months after returning. The surveys included an official explanation of the military's position regarding PTSD and the availability of treatment. Soldiers were told that there would be no stigma connected to seeking treatment and that their careers would not be affected if they did. The results of these surveys clearly indicated that one in five active duty soldiers needed psychological treatment and two in five members of the reserve components needed help. Follow-up surveys after soldiers received treatment showed that educating soldiers about PTSD, its causes and its prevention before deployment, often increased the success of treatment, and doctors were able to begin therapy much sooner with greater effectiveness. This is a major point and must be given greater emphasis. As the surveys revealed, a soldier's cooperation and assistance with the diagnosis is essential. This initial training must put to rest concerns about being stigmatized and must stress the benefits of treatment versus the consequences of a lifetime of suffering with the symptoms of PTSD or Battle Fatigue.

The challenge to be overcome by health care professionals is the usual tendency of service members to rush through these surveys and give false information. This often happens where they are asked to self-evaluate their own mental health conditions with yes or no answers. Hard experience has taught them that answering honestly or providing too much information can cause them to be pulled out of line and delayed in some way or, at worst, to be stigmatized by their unit. Interviewers must insure that the interview is effective and not a five-minute "glad-handing" welcome. They must keep in mind that many of those who suffer from Battle Fatigue are of higher rank and are experts at covering up their personal feelings while just "sucking it up" and moving on. This, again, is why education must receive greater emphasis, because without that cooperation, effective diagnosis and treatment are impossible.

The Pentagon panel's final report also contained some general findings that one would expect, such as all government agencies with budgets try very hard not to exceed them. One way the VA does this is to disapprove veterans' claims or downgrade them, whereas if sufficient money were available, claims would receive an honest and appropriate determination.

We are constantly told that the VA has taken corrective action on these operational deficiencies. However, as recently as June 6, 2008, Department of Veterans Affairs officials were again called before a senate investigating committee to answer embarrassing questions about a cover-up. The offense was a systemwide effort to limit veterans' benefits. "Last month, Dr. Norma Perez, a psychologist and coordinator at a department's clinic in central Texas, circulated an e-mail warning colleagues not to diagnose post-traumatic stress disorder in new patients too quickly, noting the growing number of 'compensation seeking veterans' coming in. There is a sense, whether it's perception or reality, that VA Officials make decisions based on money and not on whether veterans are getting the best health care they need," said Senator Patty Murray, D-Wash. "It's disconcerting when we see things like this" (*Stars and Stripes*, Pacific edition, June 6, 2008).

Additionally, the panel found that in the payment of veterans' claims, many veterans who were classified as disabled and had families with no means of support were routinely told that their first check would be mailed to them in twelve months. The panel's report also revealed the perception that the VA deals with each veteran in a very casual and "offhand" manner. Veterans seeking care are repeatedly asked for the same information, and records are often lost or misplaced. These same veterans also feel that, in determining their disability ratings, doctors are highly subjective, and it appears to the veteran that the greatest concern of the VA is not in caring for them, but in saving money. This claim is partially validated by a lack of uniformity in evaluating veterans. A veteran who is rated with a 40 percent disability in Maine can go to California and receive an 80 percent evaluation for the same disability. A standard needs to be implemented nationwide.

In the past, a soldier or Marine coming off active duty, having been diagnosed by the military with PTSD, would still need to be examined by the VA to establish that he or she really did have the condition before treatment could begin. Responding to an inquiry from U.S. Senator Daniel Akaka (D-HI), Chairman of the Veterans Affairs committee, on February 25, 2008, VA Secretary Peake directed the VA regional offices to no longer require such evidence but instead to immediately begin accepting the active duty diagnosis and start treatment as soon as possible.

On a related issue, during 2007, an investigation at Walter Reed Army Medical Center revealed that military personnel who were waiting for outpatient care or follow-up treatment were housed in substandard and, in some cases, unhealthy quarters. Wounded soldiers managed other wounded soldiers. Soldiers dealing with their own psychological disorders had been put in charge of others at risk of suicide. Disengaged clerks, unqualified platoon sergeants, and overworked case managers fumbled with simple needs: feeding soldiers' families who are close to poverty, replacing a uniform ripped off by medics, or helping a brain-damaged soldier to remember his next appointment.

"We've done our duty. We fought the war. We came home wounded. Fine! But whoever the people are back here who are supposed to give us the easy transition should be doing it," said Marine Sgt. Ryan Groves, 26, an amputee who lived at Walter Reed for sixteen months. "We don't know what to do. The people who are supposed to know don't have the answers. It's a nonstop process of stalling."

This would be bad enough, but with each platoon sergeant in charge of 125 patients, there are too many stories about lost records, missed appointments, no one managing cases, and soldiers held for months, sometimes years, seemingly lost in the system until they are discovered again. Once a soldier's tangled status is sorted out, a determination is finally made, and he or she is released to the Veterans Administration for long-term care.

A Defense Department investigation, initiated after newspaper and Congressional investigations, recommended that the army hire and train case managers who would handle no more than thirty patients. These managers would then act as guides and advocates to insure that patients don't get lost in the system and do receive the care to which they are entitled.

I recently attended a veterans' organization meeting where the benefits coordinator spoke about the work he was doing to insure that veterans receive all the care and entitlements they were due. This gentleman, an air force veteran himself, told a fantastic tale about a Missouri National Guardsman who was mobilized with a Texas National Guard unit and sent to Iraq. While in Iraq, his unit was attacked one night by enemy artillery. The soldier, along with a small group of his squad members, was caught out in the open, and they quickly dived into a shallow, sandbagged trench. Because of almost total darkness, other men jumped in on top of them and, as a result, the soldier's leg was broken. When the attack ended, the injured soldier was evacuated to the rear for treatment. This took him through Germany, through a general hospital in the United States, and finally to an active duty hospital in Texas. There, without his records, the hospital staff made a determination that, as a National Guardsman, he did not qualify for treatment of a noncombat injury. With all the soldier's advocates and inspector generals along the way, it's difficult to understand how this story could happen. But it did, and the story gets even worse. The soldier was discharged from the hospital in Texas with his leg still not treated and with no money, so he hitchhiked back to his home in Missouri. Finally, through the efforts of friends and family, the soldier did receive VA medical care for his leg, but since six months had elapsed from the time of his injury, complications had set in, and the soldier's leg had to be removed. Fortunately, this story, if true, is not typical, but the military is famous for letting soldiers slip through the cracks. Our soldiers deserve much more! As a rich nation, we must do a better job of caring for our military.

How did our health care get to this state, with the most advanced and technologically superior military in the world? Part of the answer will become obvious. In a recent visit with my thirty-one-year-old son, a veteran of service in Iraq, it was quickly apparent to me that he had not been trained to recognize or deal with Battle Fatigue. As a captain, he had commanded a tank company in the southern part of Baghdad. In a roundabout way, he told me that Battle Fatigue or PTSD was not mentioned prior to his deployment. As we talked further, he explained that, unlike other wars, troops in Iraq were not left in heavy combat for long periods of time and, in fact, most of his missions were accomplished in one day, allowing the men to be back in their quarters safe and sound every evening. He went on to say that, as a ready reaction force, his unit would often move in to secure an area where a suicide bomber had struck or to help clean up bomb debris after an attack. Their missions, he said, often exposed his men to some pretty grisly sights, and some of the men had trouble dealing with these experiences. He also related to me the story of his company 1st Sergeant getting killed by a sniper and the devastating emotional effect it had on the entire company.

My son further explained that counseling teams were located at his base and others across the country, where a soldier could go without the stigma of getting permission from his chain of command, to receive treatment or counseling for "combat stress," as they called it. The mission of these teams is to help soldiers cope with the horrors of the battlefield, so that they can return to it as soon as possible. Although these counseling teams may be available, it is left to the soldier's own initiative to seek help. The need for help is something that all battlefield leaders should closely monitor. Neither my son nor any of his subordinates had received Battle Fatigue training to recognize the symptoms, to avoid the causes, or to know where they could go to receive help for this condition.

A recent article in the *Wall Street Journal* discussed the success of many of the counseling programs mentioned above. In an interview with Lt. Gen. Kevin Kiley, the army's top medical officer, the mental health program was briefly explained. He stated that, due to the special nature of the Iraq war, repeat deployments, tight troop levels, and the mental strain on soldiers, the army had established ten combat stress centers in Iraq to help soldiers cope with psychological problems and to allow them to finish their tours.

The army's latest efforts at treatment reflect huge changes over previous wars where most soldiers were young draftees and any sort of psychological care was administered far to the rear or was only available after their discharge from the service. Today's soldiers are volunteers, which means they are older and better trained. However, the most significant change is that today's army is less than half the size of what it was during the cold war, yet the missions are greater, requiring soldiers to work more hours and do multiple tours. Because of these reduced strength levels, soldiers with traumas from their first or second tour will likely be ordered to return to the combat zone for a third and fourth tour. Psychiatrists in Iraq have found that, with repeat tours, Battle Fatigue symptoms just grow more acute.

To try to keep soldiers healthy in combat, the army has dramatically increased the number of mental-health workers in Iraq; it now stands at around three hundred, which is approximately one for every five hundred servicemen. These efforts are apparently paying off, with the number of soldiers being shipped home for psychiatric problems recently being cut in half.

The following combat story is typical of the thousands of Battle Fatigue injuries the military is experiencing today: Steve Smith is a captain in the army who flew helicopters in Iraq in a combat support role. He has returned home after sustaining a leg injury when his helicopter was shot down. Captain Smith is no longer serving on active duty but was medically discharged because of the seriousness of his injuries. Along with his physical injuries, he also suffers from various psychological injuries. His greatest concern is sleep. He fears going to sleep every night, because he has nightmares and can't shake the feeling that if he doesn't stay awake, something bad is going to happen, and he won't be able to stop it.

Captain Smith has given up on returning to the military. He's put away his uniform, his old friends have stopped coming around, and he's stopped trying to contacting them. He stays at home every day and has tried to become involved in other things, but he can't stop thinking about what he saw in Iraq and the chopper accident that happened when he was in charge. He has lost interest in flying, which is something he once loved, and is now avoiding people and living in the past.

Captain Smith is not alone; many of our returning veterans who served in Iraq or Afghanistan have also experienced at least one traumatic event there. These events can overwhelm an individual's natural coping abilities. Sometimes, just hearing about an incident involving someone you know can be a traumatic experience. Service members who have experienced a traumatic event should review the list of symptoms in Appendix C and contact the address listed there for more information.

Reports from health care workers in Afghanistan and Iraq indicate that most Battle Fatigue symptoms are the same now as in previous wars: they involve a traumatic experience mixed with anxiety, followed by nightmares that interrupt sleep, depriving soldiers of sufficient rest to function properly. This loss of sleep leads to fatigue and tension during the day and a tendency toward inattention and quick anger. Through counseling, the nightmares can often be quieted or sleep medication can be prescribed to allow the soldier or Marine to get a full night's sleep. The key seems to be for health care professionals or fellow servicemen, even family members, to get the individual to stay engaged in society, to interact with others, and especially to talk about his or her traumatic experiences. Verbalizing these issues lessens their severity. Too often, soldiers cannot face the prospect of going to sleep at night and reliving their worst nightmares, without first drugging themselves with alcohol or whatever might be available, doing further damage to their careers, families, and health. This is why leaders at the very lowest levels must be trained to recognize the symptoms of Battle Fatigue, to render proper assistance, and to make the necessary referrals.

Often in interviews with health care professionals, I'm told that PTSD cannot be cured, that only the symptoms can be reduced. Additionally, I've been told that individuals with PTSD just have to learn to live with their demons, that no cure is available. To set the record straight, modern medicine does have treatment procedures and medicines that will greatly reduce the symptoms of PTSD and, in many cases, actually cure the veteran. Below is a partial list of some of the procedures available to the up-to-date health care professional. So, no soldier or veteran should ever accept the prognosis that there is nothing that can be done to help him or her with a particular problem.

Listed are some of the latest techniques used by trained health care professionals in the treatment of PTSD:

Eye Movement Desensitization and Reprocessing

Eye Movement Desensitization and Reprocessing (EMDR) deals with stimulating the brain's right and left hemispheres through bilateral eye movement. Although it may seem like some mumbo-jumbo, hypnotic cure, the Department of Defense and the Department of Veterans Affairs strongly recommend EMDR as one of the effective treatments for PTSD. Researchers cannot explain exactly how or why EMDR works, but it does, in fact, work, they say. A practitioner directory can be found at the following Web site: http://emdria.org/.

Exposure Therapy

Exposure therapy is based on the principle that we get used to things that are just annoying and not truly dangerous. For example, if you visit a friend in a large city who lives in a second-floor apartment beside an elevated railroad, it would be very annoying every time a train screeched by, shaking the building and rattling the windows to the point that conversation became difficult. In this type of situation, you might wonder how a person could live with all that noise. If you stayed in the apartment for two weeks, you would probably not be annoyed by passing trains or not even be aware of them. Exposure therapy asks patients to confront, in a safe way, the very situations, objects, people, and memories they have attached to the trauma that they are very consciously avoiding.

Anxiety Management

Anxiety management involves learning several skills that will help you cope better with your symptoms. People usually try all of these anxiety management techniques to determine what helps most. When PTSD symptoms strike, anxiety management techniques are used to vary the intensity of symptoms and the distress they create. But it is not enough to understand the principles behind these techniques; they must be practiced repeatedly until they can be employed easily and automatically. Some people use anxiety management techniques to help control anxiety while they do exposure therapy. The following are some of the different techniques for anxiety management:

- Breathing training
- Relaxation
- Assertiveness training
- Positive thinking and self-talk
- Thought stopping

Cognitive Therapy

Cognitive therapy helps the individual understand how his thoughts influence his feelings. There are four steps to reducing negative thinking:

- Become more aware of distressing thoughts
- Pay attention to the connections between your thoughts, feelings, and behavior
- Challenge your negative thoughts
- Substitute positive thoughts for negative ones

Col. Paul D. Walker (Ret)

Supportive Counseling

All patients need and deserve support and empathetic understanding. Supportive counseling helps by shoring up defenses, utilizing strengths, minimizing weakness, explaining the characteristics and course of PTSD, monitoring changes, and reassuring the patient that improvement will occur in time. With the patient's permission and support, explain to him that his family members, friends, and others are important to his timely recovery. These individuals constitute a network of support that can sustain a person and can eventually help to resolve the issue on its own, as it often does.

Medication Therapy

In the past, medications were thought to offer very little to PTSD sufferers. This is no longer true. Unfortunately, many people who write about PTSD still have these mistaken beliefs, ignoring the sound research that exists today. There are a number of highly effective medications that can now be prescribed by your doctor.

Psychotherapy

When people develop PTSD, their beliefs about security and the predictability of life are shaken. It is as though PTSD sufferers are grieving their loss of innocence about the things they can't control and are realizing the cruel realities of life. While work and the passage of time are powerful antidotes for PTSD, some may also benefit from psychodynamic psychotherapy, focused on the unpredictability of life and the inability of society to guarantee safety. The goal of such psychotherapy is to help suffering individuals regain a balanced perspective of the risks we all face. However, according to most experts, the value of this type of treatment appears very slim at best.

Finally, the most recent and revealing example of the current degree of ignorance and lack of understanding that surrounds Battle Fatigue comes from Edward Shorter, a noted medical professor and author of *A History of Psychiatry*. In an article for *American Heritage* magazine in September 1998, he states, "Trauma has been another trap for the new psychiatry. In the 1970s, Post-Traumatic Stress Disorder (PTSD) was first articulated by a group of Vietnam veterans, and it rapidly disseminated from the narrow world of maladjusted and unhappy vets to the wide world in which stress and unhappiness are as common as grass. Suddenly, the normal frictions and disappointments of life became a psychiatric illness and PTSD counseling, a growth industry." To cloud the issue even further, some members of the psychiatric community claim that there is no such condition as Battle Fatigue or Post Traumatic Stress Disorder. They contend that events as stressful as the Holocaust produced no particular pattern of psychiatric illness in its victims, nor did the conditions many American POW's endured in the European Theatre during World War II. So they regard modern day claimants of these conditions with suspicion.

These biased and prejudicial remarks reveal the size of the challenge to educate and inform the public and health care workers about the very real and legitimate effects of Battle Fatigue, often referred to as PTSD; hopefully, this book will help in that effort.

CHAPTER FIVE

Stories from the Front Line

The *Stars and Stripes* newspaper is a soldier's hometown paper while he's overseas. It's printed daily and helps the military stay up to date on national events and also contains articles about the issues that affect the day-to-day lives of our men and women in uniform.

In order for news to be credible, soldiers must feel comfortable with the source of their information and advice. *Stars and Stripes* is familiar to most military personnel and their families, and its manner of presentation is both believable and trusted. This unique newspaper has been delivered worldwide since the beginning of World War II, right out to the most remote frontline positions, wherever American military personnel are deployed. Its reporters have always had wide access to our servicemen and servicewomen, no matter how remote or dangerous their location.

As a longtime reader of the *Stars and Stripes*, I've noticed the paper's thorough and progressive coverage of Battle Fatigue. This coverage gives a very clear picture of the current challenges facing the military and how they're addressing them to date.

The following is a representative sample or summary of those well-written "frontline" articles, used with permission from the *Stars and*

Stripes. These articles show, in a very sensitive manner, the seriousness of Battle Fatigue and the various ways the military has chosen to deal with it. (Appendix B has a complete list, with the full text of these "*Stripes*" articles that deal with psychological injuries.)

For many years, I have been sadly aware of both active duty soldiers and veterans who have suffered from psychological injuries that resulted from military service. My reaction has always been one of sincere respect and gratitude for the individual having sacrificed his health in service to our country. But there has been a degree of pity, too, because I knew that in virtually all instances the individuals would carry their injuries for the remainder of their lives. I've even heard the doctor's stern diagnosis, "there's nothing more we can do for you, you're just going to have to live with this condition." Now, as outlined in the following article, military medicine, using EMDR, has progressed to the point where we talk in terms of not just treatment but an actual cure for some forms of Battle Fatigue or PTSD.

Seeing Relief from Post-traumatic Stress: Therapists Trained in Eye Movement Desensitization and Reprocessing at Landstuhl

by Steve Mraz, Mideast edition *Stars and Stripes*, August 7, 2007

During the past few weeks, about a dozen social workers, psychologists, and other mental health professionals at Landstuhl, Germany, have been trained to perform a treatment called eye movement desensitization and reprocessing. Developed in the late 1980s by psychologist Francine Shapiro, eye movement desensitization and reprocessing, or EMDR, deals with stimulating the brain's right and left hemispheres through bilateral movement. That bilateral movement usually comes in the form of patients following a therapist's fingers back and forth with their eyes. With patients told to recall a painful memory while moving their eyes back and forth, EMDR may seem like some mumbo-jumbo, hypnotic cure. But the Department of Defense and the Department of Veterans Affairs strongly recommend EMDR as one of four treatments that work for PTSD in military and nonmilitary populations. The procedure is one of several standard therapies being used by counselors at Walter Reed Army Medical Center in Washington, D.C. "The treatment, during which patients are fully awake and alert, produces positive results that can be demonstrated," said Dr. John Hartung. "It's much more than moving your eyes while thinking of a disturbing thought," he said. Researchers cannot explain exactly how or why EMDR works, but it does work, they say. Brain scans of patients recalling a traumatic memory show a lopsided image, Hartung explained. "The parts of the brain responsible for negative emotions and protecting us from danger in emergencies are highly active. The portions of the brain that control positive emotions, language and common sense are basically shut down," Hartung said.

"You put that all together, and you've got a person under trauma overreacting to innocuous stimuli," he said. "Now, here's the really good news. We can't tell you exactly how we get there, but we know where we get. Four and a half hours later with EMDR treatment, we take a picture of that person's brain. As the person thinks of that trauma now, it's no longer traumatic. The brain is flashing on both sides, nicely balanced."

The 4½ hours come from three 90-minute sessions typical with EMDR treatment. Despite evidence in research and journal articles that EMDR works, some people still do not use the technique, Hartung said. The question is, Why isn't it being used more?" He said, "This is the best we have for helping people recover from the wounds of combat and move back to civilian life."

"Military Aims to Remove Stigma from Seeking Therapy for Post-combat Stress,"

This summary of an article by Nancy Montgomery, touches on one of the major factors that keep soldiers from seeking treatment:

Although the military has moved into the twenty-first century with its weapons and technology, some of its attitudes and prejudices remain rooted in the nineteenth century. I'm including all the armed services and their policies and procedures as they pertain to PTSD and other psychological injuries. As an example, the attitude toward blood injuries is very direct and straightforward; a soldier is wounded, we "fix him up" or treat his wounds, and return him to duty with a Purple Heart and new status as a combat hero who has been tested and survived. If his injuries are too severe, he's awarded his Purple Heart and transferred to the VA for care, but with a certain positive status. If, on the other hand, a soldier has a psychological injury due to prolonged exposure to combat, he's treated differently. First, the soldier is treated with suspicion that his condition is not legitimate, that he's just trying to get out of harm's way. The soldier is also looked upon as letting his unit down, and now someone else is going to have to perform his duties. Additionally, the chain of command will see him as weak and unreliable and not able to be trusted with greater responsibility. His efficiency report may directly or indirectly reflect this attitude. As further evidence of institutional prejudice, the military awards no Purple Hearts for this type of injury, and if the condition is documented in one's medical records, he or she will normally be disqualified from obtaining a security clearance or sensitive assignment. These are just a few of the obvious hurdles that must be addressed, but there are many more subtle acts of prejudice and discrimination that the soldier who reports a psychological injury will quickly experience. This fine article attempts to address some of the stigma or expectation of stigma that accompanies these injuries.

"Special Team in Iraq Combats Stress, Not Insurgents"

by Sandra Jontz

This article deals with the problems of access to mental health treatment for frontline soldiers. In past wars, psychological treatment has only been available far to the rear in field hospitals. Soldiers, usually suffering from Battle Fatigue, never feel stressed enough or traumatized enough to make the long trip back to the rear area, unless they are an extreme or severe casualty. Part of the reason for this is that they have a medic in the unit to handle the "small stuff."

To address this situation, mental health care providers have been going out to frontline units and sharing their hardships as they live with soldiers who actually do the fighting. For example, they stand guard duty, fill sandbags, and go out on patrol in order to gain the confidence and trust of these soldiers and get them to talk about anything that might be causing stress. There is a realization that soldiers feel they will be stigmatized for seeking treatment. But by interacting with these mental health care workers on their own turf, it's perceived as OK to talk about how the war's going or how they're holding up under the stress of combat.

This program has been successful, but there are still hurdles to overcome. After all of the attention this subject has received, there are still commanders who object to having mental health care workers visit their units. Their concerns are filled with the age-old prejudices that health care workers have had to deal with over the years. These include concerns that the unit as a whole will be perceived as weak or "not up to the task." Further, if health care workers were allowed in, then this would cause "good soldiers" to start complaining about symptoms, real or imagined. Often, health care workers sit down with commanders and try to explain that they are actually "force multipliers"—that is, a means for keeping more soldiers healthy and "fit for duty" and for increasing the odds that the commanders will return with all their soldiers.

Mental health personnel were first embedded in units in 2003, when the Army Surgeon General became concerned about the rapid increase in suicides within deployed units. As a measure of their success, those units that allowed mental health workers in saw a dramatic decrease in both the number of suicides and of psychological injuries.

Number of Veterans Seeking Treatment for Stress Has Doubled

by Leo Shane III, Mideast edition,
Stars and Stripes, November 2, 2006

WASHINGTON—The number of Iraq and Afghanistan veterans getting treatment for post-traumatic stress nearly doubled from the fall of 2005 to this summer, but officials from the Department of Veterans Affairs say that isn't necessarily bad news.

They believe the increase points to a growing awareness of the symptoms of PTSD and a larger willingness among young veterans to seek out help for the illness.

According to internal department data, the number of young veterans receiving PTSD treatment from VA hospitals and counseling centers rose from 20,394 patients in September 2005, to 38,144 patients in June 2006, an increase of 87 percent.

Hospital cases alone totaled 29,041 in June, up 82 percent from nine months earlier. The number of veterans who visited counseling centers more than doubled, from 4,467 to 9,103 over that same period.

Dr. Ira Katz, VA deputy chief of patient mental health services, said, "At least some of that increase is due to the increasing number of veterans: The number of troops who have separated from the service since September 2002, grew to 588,923 this summer, up more than 150,000 from the previous year."

But Alfonso Batres, chief officer for the department's readjustment services, says he thinks most of the jump in the number of cases is directly related to outreach efforts over the last few years.

Overall, the number of Iraq and Afghanistan veterans visiting VA centers for any type of counseling rose from 43,682 in September 2005, to 144,227 in November 2006.

"We've really concentrated our efforts on reaching these troops," he said, "and now we're seeing more and more of them coming to the counseling centers."

The VA has been emphasizing stress disorders and their symptoms through public campaigns and information given to troops before they leave the military.

Batres said that, in addition, for the last two years about one hundred VA workers—all retired military personnel who served in Iraq and Afghanistan—have been stationed at demobilization sites overseas to talk about PTSD and veterans benefits for troops, to give them a better idea of what to expect after they leave the services.

"There is no one better to let (troops) know about that than their fellow peers," Batres said. "They're really getting the message out."

Batres also said the Defense Department's post-deployment mental health assessment, now repeated three to six months after troops return from combat tours overseas, has also greatly raised awareness of PTSD and its symptoms.

Officer Sees "Perfect Storm" Brewing in Military's Mental Health Care System

by Allison Batdorff, Pacific edition,
Stars and Stripes, September 22, 2006

YOKOSUKA NAVAL BASE, JAPAN—Gaps in care, combined with the stress of combat in Iraq and Afghanistan, are creating a "perfect storm" within the U.S. military mental health system, according to a navy commander who spoke at Yokosuka Naval Base on Wednesday.

Mark Russell, a child psychologist and director of educational and development intervention services for bases across Japan, painted a picture of unmet needs and unrecognized opportunity stemming from the global war on terrorism.

"We are in a crisis situation," Russell said. "And it's going to get worse. We're making progress but are far from making good on our promise to provide the best mental health care possible for the men and women we send to war," Russell told the gathering.

More than fifty-six thousand troops, or 10 percent, have returned from Iraq and Afghanistan with a mental health diagnosis, making up a third of those in Veterans Affairs care. The cost of mental health care is high, he said. The VA spent $4.3 billion on post-traumatic stress disorder alone in 2004.

Also, of the 9,145 (out of a possible 178,644) veterans who showed signs of PTSD between 2001 and 2004, only 22 percent were referred on to mental health care. "That creates a chasm between a need for care and actually getting it," Russell said.

Another gap falls between DOD guidelines for mental health treatment and the training given to mental health workers, he said.

"Out of 133 mental health providers I surveyed, 90 percent of them had no training in the top four treatments the DOD recommends for PTSD," Russell said.

"There also are problems with leadership, high burnout rates among caregivers, and the tendency to treat those suffering from hyperarousal compared to those who dissociate," he said.

"The bottom line is that we have increased demand and fewer resources to meet that demand. But the DOD has made significant strides, especially in terms of frontline combat mental health care," he added. The military's PIES system, basing combat mental health care on Proximity, Immediacy, Expectancy, and Simplicity, is working," he said.

"The numbers of mental health workers on the front lines is unprecedented, " Russell said. "This is an all-out effort."

"More troops are using frontline mental health services, with 40 percent getting help in 2005 compared to 29 percent in 2004. And, most importantly, 90 percent of those who get frontline help return to duty," he said.

"The DOD also has improved screening programs, has established deployment centers with quality information, is conducting more surveys, and is getting more information out to veterans after they come home," Russell said.

"But the DOD could be doing more for the troops, caregivers, and for combat mental health in terms of treating the 'invisible wounds of warfare,'" he said.

"Right now, the DOD is in a historically unique position to lead the world in understanding, assessment, prevention, and treatment," Russell said. "Have we advanced science?"

"The military has a love/hate relationship with mental health care," he added. "We like it in war and know that increased mental health is a force multiplier," Russell said. "But in peacetime, mental health falls to the low end of the totem pole."

"It's up to the military health professionals today to 'take up the sword.' I've already turned in my retirement paperwork," he said.

Army Takes Aim at Post-traumatic Stress [summary]

by Joseph Giordono, Pacific edition,
Stars and Stripes, June 18, 2004

YONGSAN GARRISON, SOUTH KOREA—The 121st General Hospital plans to hold a two-day summit of medical personnel in South Korea in coming weeks specifically to address stress disorders. And the hospital plans to start a stress management group for soldiers and leaders at bases here.

"At least from the psychiatric standpoint, the army is really responding to this," Gabriel said.

Though by no means a new disorder, PTSD first was codified in the early 1980s and added to the *Diagnostic and Statistical Manual of Mental Disorders*, which the military uses as its guide for mental health issues.

Persons exposed to life-threatening or shocking events can experience a range of symptoms, from mild temporary reactions to complex PTSD. Stress disorders have clear biological and psychological symptoms and very specific diagnoses, mental health professionals said.

According to the National Center for Post-traumatic Stress Disorder, "about 30 percent of the men and women who have spent time in war zones experience PTSD. An additional 20–25 percent have had partial PTSD at some point in their lives."

A national study of American civilians conducted in 1995 estimated that the lifetime prevalence of PTSD was 5 percent in men and 10 percent in women.

The numbers peaked with more than half of all male Vietnam veterans and almost half of all female Vietnam veterans having experienced "clinically serious stress reaction symptoms." Studies estimate the numbers at 8 percent of Gulf War I veterans; no data is yet available for the current Iraq conflict, officials said.

The center's site also includes *The Iraq War Clinician Guide, 2nd Edition*, which details the different circumstances, military policies, and potential stressors being faced by soldiers now deployed.

That guide details post-battle debriefings under a system called PIES: Proximity-Immediacy-Expectancy-Simplicity.

"Early intervention is provided close to a soldier's unit, as soon as possible," the clinician's guide says. "Soldiers are told that their experience is normal and they can expect to return to their unit shortly. They are also provided simple interventions to counteract 'fatigue' (e.g., 'three hots and a cot')."

"The point here is that soldiers who experience severe war-zone stress reactions likely will have received some sort of special care. On the other hand, it is without question stigmatizing for soldiers to share fear and doubt and to reveal signs of reduced capacity. This is especially true in the modern, all-volunteer military, with many soldiers looking to enhance their careers."

Thus, the *Clinician's Guide* states, some veterans who don't exhibit signs of PTSD until later "will have suffered silently and may still feel a great need not to show vulnerability because of peer pressure."

Medical officials at the 121st Hospital agree there are many things that can be done while on deployment to help counter development of stress-related disorders.

In addition to the "three hots and a cot," Major Sheila Adams and Major Geoffrey Gabriel, two experienced mental healthcare workers said, "things as simple as talking with other unit members or chaplains after an engagement could help." Again, they said, the willingness and cooperation of unit commanders and NCOs to acknowledge potential cases would be crucial in early detection and treatment.

Col. Paul D. Walker (Ret)

Sigonella Team Helped Cole Sailors Deal with Stress, Grief

by Anthony Burgos, European edition,
Stars and Stripes, November 1, 2000

NAVAL AIR STATION SIGONELLA, SICILY—Saving the USS Cole from sinking was the crew's first battle after a bomb ripped a 40-foot by 40-foot hole into the ship's hull. Saving the Cole's crew from the blast's echo and clearing smoke after the attack was the mission of the Special Intervention Response Team (SIRT) from the naval hospital in Sigonella, Sicily.

The October 12 explosion crippled the billion-dollar destroyer, killed seventeen sailors and wounded thirty-nine. And while the wounded have returned to the States, the almost three hundred remaining sailors had their own battles to face, some aboard the ship, others inside their heads.

"Imagine being one of the victims of the Oklahoma City bombing and having to live in the destroyed building," said Lt. Silvetti, who is part of the eight-person team that deployed to Aden, Yemen, two days after the attack. "That's what conditions were like when we got there."

The SIRT team, comprised of personnel from different medical fields, has a straightforward mission regarding the Cole: counsel the traumatized service-members. According to Chief Petty Officer Don Posson, a SIRT member sent to the USS Cole, that's why they got the call.

Posson said that as soon as they arrived in Yemen, they had a lot of work to do: "Most of the injured had already been evacuated, and the medical staff from the ship and Bahrain had been working hard. So, we helped sailors that were going through the grief cycle."

While sailors worked long hours to keep the ship afloat, they also had to deal with the shock of the attack. Many were experiencing nightmares, sleeplessness, vomiting, and lack of appetite.

"Some of them were so traumatized that they wouldn't sleep on the inside of the ship," Silvetti said. "These were all normal reactions to such a tragic event."

According to Posson, the team split up by rank to work with sailors at different levels.

By talking to sailors before and after their work shifts, the team would assess how things were going. "It was hard because we are outsiders. But we would ask people to speak about what they were going through and to look out for each other," Silvetti said.

"Once the sailors realized that they were all experiencing the same stress-related illnesses, they took less time to recuperate and get back to the mission of saving their ship," Silvetti said.

Although most people take days or longer to rebound, the team had to make sure the process was accelerated, Silvetti said. Some sailors were prescribed sleeping medication. Others were coached on ways to combat stress and fatigue. "We told them to get sleep, no matter what time of day," he added.

Lieutenant Joe Taylor, another SIRT member, said the crew's resiliency pulled them through the traumatic times. "They took a hit and still came back to save the ship," he said. "Their comradery will always stand out in my mind."

The vast majority of people who live through a life-changing event will be able to handle the stress that follows. But not everyone is so lucky.

"Statistically, 80 percent of people who go through a trauma of this type recover completely," Silvetti said. "It was the other 20 percent we had to help manage the stress. By the time we left, they were good to go."

As a matter of fact, Silvetti said that the Cole's career counselor said the crew's attitude toward the ship and the navy may have changed after the fatal assault.

"Prior to the explosion, there weren't many sailors re-enlisting," Silvetti said. "But while we were there, we saw three re-enlistment ceremonies, and we were told that thirteen others were scheduled. They were proud of being members of the USS Cole team."

The USS Cole was towed from the Aden on Sunday and is in the process of loading onto a Norwegian heavy-lift ship, the Blue Marlin. A group of sailors, engineers, and security personnel will travel on the Blue Marlin during its five-week trip to the United States.

Soldiers Need Tougher Psychological, Emotional Training, Says Infantry Head

European edition, *Stars and Stripes*, June 15, 2002

"Today's soldier needs tougher psychological and emotional training for battle," the Army's Chief of Infantry said at the annual Infantry Conference in Atlanta on Tuesday, the *Atlanta Journal and Constitution* reported.

Major General Paul Eaton said, "The army does a good job of preparing soldiers physically, but dedicates 'the least amount of time to psychological and emotional readiness,'" according to the report.

"Infantry soldiers should receive rigorous training, similar to what Army Rangers go through, that tests their ability to withstand stress while also testing their judgment, values, confidence, and perseverance," Eaton said.

Such training would be expensive, Eaton was reported as saying. A possible model for such training is available from the Army Ranger school.

As an example of the psychological challenges young soldiers face, Eaton noted the dual roles of diplomat carrying out national policy and soldier ready to respond to attack, that troops sent on peacekeeping missions must play, the paper reported.

Military Health Officials Trying to Keep Pace with War's Mental Toll: Alcoholism Common for Those Afflicted with PTSD

By Matt Millham, European edition,
Stars and Stripes, July 16, 2006

As an army computer specialist, Brian didn't expect to find himself in combat in Iraq. But two months after arriving in Baghdad, while on patrol with a cavalry unit, he faced his first of many brushes with death when a makeshift bomb exploded near his vehicle.

"That scared the (expletive) out of me," said Brian, which is not his real name. As a member of Alcoholics Anonymous who recently completed mandatory treatment for alcohol and drug abuse problems, he spoke on condition he wouldn't have to give his name.

Brian didn't realize his clashes on the battlefield had mentally scarred him, but memories of what he went through put him in a state of perpetual anxiety. After returning from Iraq, he dealt with his anxiety the same way many Vietnam veterans did and still do: He turned to alcohol and drugs.

Substance abuse often goes hand-in-hand with post-traumatic stress disorder, a psychiatric condition that affects roughly 15 percent of Vietnam veterans and perhaps as much as 17 percent of Iraq veterans including, doctors say, Brian. The condition often occurs after experiencing or witnessing life-threatening events.

Soon after the war in Iraq started, the Department of Defense began screening returning combat vets for evidence of mental health issues so troubled troops could get help as soon as possible. The army also sent mental health professionals downrange to check on the quality of care troops were getting. The hope is that these efforts will keep new vets from suffering the mental health and substance abuse problems that plague Vietnam vets. If they fail, the result could look a lot like Brian did before treatment.

Having slipped through the PTSD screening process, Brian dulled his anxiety with a self-prescribed regimen of alcohol and drugs. His heavy drinking and risky behavior got him two charges of drunken driving in less than seven months.

"It wasn't until I got my second DWI that I was ready to admit I had a problem," he said.

He was about to get promoted to sergeant, but instead was busted down to private, sentenced to forty-five days of extra duty and restriction, and had to forfeit pay. He was also ordered into the army substance abuse program.

It was only after his mental health had thrown his career on the rocks that doctors said he likely suffered from PTSD.

After the diagnosis, he was enrolled in a six-week, inpatient treatment program at Landstuhl Regional Medical Center in Landstuhl, Germany, that helped him deal with his dependence on alcohol and drugs and identify the events that had driven him to substance abuse.

"They did a great job with getting me the help I needed," Brian said.

If substance abuse among Iraq vets with PTSD follows the course of Vietnam vets, more than 13 percent of troops returning from Iraq with mental health issues could be expected to find themselves in Brian's shoes, as they face alcohol or other substance abuse problems.

"I think a lot of that information is still coming in," Kate Azar, the clinical director of Darmstadt, Germany's army substance abuse program, said. "That is something we are definitely keeping an eye on."

The DOD's efforts to rein in mental health problems among combat vets, though robust compared with those from any previous U.S. armed conflict, aren't going far enough for some.

In May, the Government Accountability Office filed a report that said only one out of every five troops who screened positive for PTSD upon leaving a war zone was referred for follow-up evaluations. But those in the military have been more optimistic about the mitigating effects of the mental health care now afforded troops.

A January 2005, report chartered by the U.S. Army Surgeon General said mental health and well-being improved from the first to the second year of the Iraq war. The report included troops stationed throughout the Middle East, including those in noncombat roles in places such as Kuwait and Qatar.

According to the report, 18 percent of troops screened positive for mental health issues during the first year of the war in Iraq. The number dropped to 13 percent among those who served during the second year of the war.

The Army has continued to monitor troops' health, and in November, a mental health advisory team finished looking at troops in the third Iraq rotation. What the team concludes might provide some insight into what happens when troops are sent back into the fray.

"The world is speculating that PTSD will be higher among troops who have been to Iraq more than once," said Col. Elspeth Ritchie, a psychiatry consultant to the Army Surgeon General.

If mental health issues among vets of Iraq and Afghanistan are on the rise, programs such as the army substance abuse program could soon find themselves overwhelmed.

Among Vietnam veterans seeking treatment for PTSD, 60–80 percent have alcohol use disorders, according to a fact sheet from the U.S. Department of Veterans Affairs' National Center for PTSD.

Robert McCollum, who runs the army substance abuse program for the Installation Management Agency-Europe, said the program's offices across the continent are already feeling the pressure. "My people are busy. Their plates are full," he said.

Col. Paul D. Walker (Ret)

Troops' Health Woes Run Gamut from "Saddam's Revenge" to Severe Stress

by Marni McEntee, European edition,
Stars and Stripes, October 29, 2003

BAGHDAD, Iraq—In Iraq's harsh environment, even soldiers safe inside their base camp face dangers.

Between combat casualties and accident victims in Iraq, medical personnel are also busy fighting microscopic enemies that can lay a troop nearly as low as a gunshot wound.

With ailments ranging from "Saddam's revenge" stomach bugs to infections caused by bad hygiene, hundreds of soldiers are lining up at sick call instead of patrolling front lines.

Some maladies are caused by a witch's brew of dust, heat, exotic bacteria, and vermin. Others stem from poor sanitation and close living quarters, said Capt. Jolene Lea, a community health nurse at the 28th Combat Support Hospital in Baghdad.

Still others are related to the stress of seeing a friend killed in battle or hearing bad news from home, Lea said. Those can manifest themselves into mental health problems and sometimes, suicide.

"The most serious illness and injury cases are evacuated from Iraq to Landstuhl Regional Medical Center in Germany. As of last week, Landstuhl doctors have treated 7,381 from Operation Iraqi Freedom, hospital spokeswoman Marie Shaw said. Only 10 percent of those casualties were from battle injuries, she said."

The problems have some troops at bases from Basra in the south to Mosul in the north afraid that living and working in Iraq may be bad for their health.

"I am very worried about the long-term health effects of this environment," Sgt. Brian Rau, of the 372nd Military Police Company in Hillah, wrote on a *Stars and Stripes* survey form. *Stripes* reporters surveyed nearly two thousand troops throughout the country in August.

"The food is bad and not reliable, so we eat on the local market every day," Rau wrote. "There is standing sewage outside our building. And the cans we use for toilets are prefilled with diesel fuel so we sit on top of those fumes daily."

Corporal Joshua Enos, a UH-60 Black Hawk crew chief who lived at an old Iraqi fighter base west of Qayaira, worried about the effects of a massive fire that broke out in a nearby sulfur plant shortly after the 101st Airborne Division took over the base in April. The fire spewed noxious black smoke into the air for days.

"Just walking out to the Humvee, I thought I was going to hyperventilate and die," Enos said. "It got so bad we were putting on our protective masks for awhile. I don't even want to know what the long-term health effects of that are going to be."

Before deploying to the Middle East, most troops were briefed on the types of health issues they would face, Lea said.

Some conditions, such as an outbreak of pneumonia, were unexpected.

In all, ninety-eight troops from Iraq were diagnosed with pneumonia, and nineteen became so ill they had to be placed on a ventilator and evacuated, said Virginia Stephanakis, a spokeswoman for the Army Surgeon General's office. Two soldiers died.

Lea and other medical personnel from troop clinics to battalion aid stations, however, say the incidence of serious illness or injury in Iraq is proportionate to the population size.

"It's not like we're coming here and seeing things we don't see at home," said Maj. Bill Dixon, a physician at the 28th CSH. "I think the soldiers are holding up pretty well," Dixon said.

The following is a sample of the more common health problems in Iraq treated by military doctors at the 28th Combat Support Hospital:

eye injuries. Dust and windblown debris are the main culprits of eye abrasions. Doctors also have treated troops who have viral conjunctivitis.

fevers. Caused by inhalation of barnyard dust contaminated by a bacteria found in herd animals such as sheep and goats. Illness causes fever, sore throat, chills, nausea, vomiting, diarrhea, and chest pain.

gastrointestinal problems. Caused by tainted food or water. In June 2006, doctors treated a number of cases of Norwalk virus, a contagious stomach flu caused by ingesting food or water contaminated with fecal matter.

gynecological problems. Poor hygiene, stress, and other factors can cause female soldiers' menstrual cycles to stop or can cause infections. Several females also have been treated for breast masses.

heat injuries. Caused by dehydration, electrolyte abnormalities, and low sodium and potassium levels. At least one soldier in Iraq has died from heatstroke.

kidney stones. Caused by the inability to metabolize certain minerals in the bloodstream. Doctors at Landstuhl Regional Medical Center in Germany said cases may be caused by soldiers not drinking enough water or by drinking water with high mineral content.

leishmaniasis. Caused by the bite from a parasite-infected sand fly. Serious cases need to be treated by a long course of antibiotics. Walter Reed Army Medical Center in Washington DC has treated twenty-two cases and the Armed Services Blood Program office has deferred troops returning from Iraq from donating blood for one year because of the problem.

orthopedic injuries. Including hernias, sprained ankles, and broken bones.

psychiatric problems. Ranging from Battle Fatigue to "adjustment disorders," to more serious mental health issues that lead to suicide.

The army is investigating twenty-one incidents of possible suicides and several other unexplained deaths.

respiratory illnesses. Dust, cigarette smoking, and pollution have contributed to an increase in asthma and bronchitis. At least ninety-eight soldiers have been diagnosed with pneumonia, and two soldiers have died from the condition.

swollen lymph nodes. Sometimes caused by an infected insect bite or other infections.

tuberculosis exposure. The illness is most common among enemy prisoners of war, but some soldiers have been exposed. Soldiers are routinely tested for tuberculosis exposure following deployments.

urological problems. Testicular masses and epididymitis, or an infection of the entrance to the urethra, caused by poor hygiene such as not changing underwear or showering regularly.

CHAPTER SIX

Summary and Recommendations

In concluding this discussion of Battle Fatigue, it must be recognized that service in the defense of our great nation is a noble and worthy occupation. It is also a dangerous one that requires the individual, from time to time, to place himself into situations where he could be killed or seriously wounded. When this happens, our grateful nation should do everything in its power to assist the soldier and his family to the fullest extent possible. However, as with anything, we can do better, and in the case of those killed or wounded, we should examine every instance for the causes and circumstances to prevent future occurrences. Battle Fatigue is one of those hard-to-define illnesses where the conditions of battle and the harsh realities of service combine to produce serious but often subtle casualties. As concerned citizens, we must do everything we can to find ways to prevent or lessen its effects. So in the interest of reducing these numbers to the lowest levels possible, the following recommendations are offered:

1. **EDUCATION:** In the past, army planners have been too preoccupied with Economy of Force operations that expose a small force to extreme combat for prolonged periods of time while they struggle to accomplish their mission. The military needs to fully understand the

consequences to the mental health of these undersized forces. This is why the senior leadership of the armed forces, starting with the Secretary of Defense on down, needs to be informed through regular briefings and seminars of the seriousness of Battle Fatigue and the need to plan for and allow for sufficient force levels to limit the instances of this condition. Further, add classes to the curriculum of all service schools, from Officer's Basic and Noncommissioned Officers (NCO) Basic to the War Colleges on this subject, so that junior leaders and senior leaders can recognize the symptoms of this condition and get help for those they lead. (The Surgeon General's Mental Health Advisory Team Report, dated 14 February 2008, makes the same recommendation). By educating NCOs and officers as to the genuine aspects of this illness, soldiers, sailors, and Marines can be made to understand that it is acceptable to seek treatment for this legitimate condition and lift the stigma that often accompanies a service member's efforts to get help. Seeking help does not mean a warrior is weak, nor a coward. These things have nothing to do with their symptoms.

2. **RECRUITING THE FORCE;** The military should spend more time choosing the type of men and women recruited into the armed services. This would limit the number of problems for commanders and, later, it would limit the cost to the Veterans Administration. History has taught us to recognize the type of individuals who will perform well in military service and those who won't. Many of those who later suffer from Battle Fatigue should never have been brought into the service to begin with. At most armed forces recruiting stations, every month, there is a rush to meet recruiting quotas. The careers of officers and NCOs often depend upon the total numbers brought in, and this pressure to meet the numbers leads to overzealous efforts by some to cut corners or look the

other way when shortcomings appear. These energetic and innovative recruiters can easily obtain waivers for or trim requirements for marginal candidates who then find themselves in uniform and totally unfit to face the rigors of combat. Recent figures indicate that over half of the recruits who require a waiver fail to complete basic training, and those with waivers who do finish training are more prone to develop Battle Fatigue. Records also indicate that the numbers of those coming in using a waiver have more than doubled since 2006. Our senior leadership should stop this practice of cutting corners on the quality of recruits. Instead, they should require services to appeal to the proper instincts of patriotism and service to country in our young men and women and then to make sure that the recruits are paid a decent salary for the dangerous jobs they perform. The military will then have all the suitable recruits it requires.

3. **MANNING LEVELS;.** The following needs to be said as loudly as I can possibly say it on paper. While the nation continues to wage two wars in the Middle East, with the very real prospect of starting a third, it is vital to the health and welfare of our armed forces and to its ability to accomplish the mission, that the size of our military be increased. This is necessary when our national command authority from the president on down regularly proclaims that the nation will maintain a presence in that part of the world for the foreseeable future. This, despite the fact that the regular army and Marine Corps are showing clear signs of exhaustion and do not currently have the resources on hand to complete their present assignments. If these missions are to be continued and success is the objective, then both components must be increased significantly. Now for an issue at a much lower level. The chapter entitled "Stories from the Front Line" mentions that mental health personnel often visit units and attempt to talk with combat soldiers about Battle Fatigue.

Remembering my own experience in a troop unit, when anyone from outside the unit came to visit with us or interview us about anything, we were always guarded in talking with them either openly or privately. I'm sure today's military is no different, and if a mental health team came in to talk with soldiers in Iraq or Afghanistan about any psychological problems, very few, if any, would admit that they had a problem or would even listen to advice about battle stress. Taking the soldiers or Marines outside of the unit for interviews or requiring a soldier to go through his chain of command would also cause him to feel that he was going to be stigmatized for needing to seek psychological help. It is also common knowledge that these interviews or therapy sessions are recorded in a soldier's medical file and usually stay there for future reference or as a basis for later VA claims or treatment. Overlooked in this effort to treat soldiers for or protect them from Battle Fatigue is the unit medic. Part of his responsibility is to prepare men and women physically and mentally for battle and to treat them if they become casualties. The combat medic is familiar to most, trusted by all, and is usually held in very high regard. This is a key individual who can diagnosis a cold and issue aspirin, bandage a serious head wound, or remove a splinter; he is one of them. His training is designed to save lives and ease suffering, while keeping soldiers healthy to fight. Preventing and treating Battle Fatigue could easily be added to his list of duties. By adding psychological training to his medic school training, this individual would be ideally placed in the unit. He would be able to discuss Battle Fatigue with soldiers and their leaders before, during, and after battles, to insure that symptoms were recognized and dealt with, down at the lowest levels. (The latest Surgeons General's MHAT 5, 14 February 2008, report, makes this same recommendation.) There would, of course, always be extreme cases, and for these, the combat medic would be well placed to recognize them and get the individual evacuated to a level of care that could help him. Our long military history has shown that organization and manning tables are very slow to change and they even resist change. But rather than an immediate sweeping change for all combat units, I would propose something the military does well—that is, start with testing a brigade or division with combat medics who have received Battle Fatigue training and then compare the results with other units to determine if the additional training for medics has reduced the number of men reporting for sick-call and the number of suicides and acts of misconduct. Although not all would be related to Battle Fatigue, a controlled test would show the effectiveness of the additional training. The bright side of this experiment would be fewer broken lives, more men fit for duty, happier families, and fewer claims for psychological treatment through the Veterans Administration. Additionally, once units are committed to the battle, senior leaders must insure that strength levels are properly maintained and that missions assigned are within the capability of the unit. Often, as strength levels decrease because of casualties and rotations, losses are not made up, and the missions are not adjusted accordingly, which opens the door to Battle Fatigue.

4. **USE OF GUARD AND RESERVE UNITS:** Our nation must be more cautious and limited in the overseas employment of its Reserve Components. Any call-up of the Guard and Reserve causes a tremendous amount of disruption in the lives of these civilian patriots. These troops must never be used on a regular basis as full-time soldiers, except in the gravest of situations. One of the great errors in the current Iraqi war is the routine call-up of Reserve and National Guard units. The regular forces exist for full-time employment to handle the nation's military needs.

The Guard and Reserve should only be called up and deployed overseas in the gravest of situations, when the nation itself is imperiled, and the entire country should then be asked to sacrifice along with the military forces. It must be remembered that these men and women did not sign up to be full-time soldiers, that most are older than active duty soldiers and more established in their civilian careers, and the military is not their primary occupation. Consideration should also be given to the fact that these civilian soldiers are policemen, firemen, teachers, city employees, and other key individuals in many of the small towns and cities across America and cannot be easily replaced for long deployments. Additionally, the tremendous stress that is placed upon these dual-status troops is magnified by multiple tours, which greatly increase their chances of becoming Battle Fatigue casualties. With the recent "surge" in Iraq that dramatically increased the size of the force, planners took the easy way out by just extending the tours of Guard and Reserve units already in-country. This shortsightedness caused the stress levels of these Reserve component soldiers to skyrocket, because of their family commitments, job arrangements, community obligations, and personal plans. If the senior leadership of the armed forces was really serious about reducing Battle Fatigue, then they would not be so reckless with the psychological health of these fine soldiers.

5. **UNIT ROTATION:** The perception of unfairness in assignments heightens the chances for Battle Fatigue. This same principal applies to individuals within a unit. There are not many cases of company clerks or others far behind the front lines suffering from Battle Fatigue. The victims of this condition are usually those who make contact with the enemy to kill or capture him. The solution is to spread the exposure to great danger among various units. If one particular unit has suffered heavy casualties, then on the next deployment, assign

that unit to a quiet area. It is a proven fact that the platoon or company that is always out front will suffer the most Battle Fatigue casualties. During the past several months, there has been heavy news coverage of U.S. Army units in Iraq that have spent their entire twelve-month to fifteen-month tours escorting supply convoys. Daily, these convoys travel over roads planted with roadside bombs and littered with the wreckage of war. The men and women who crew the armed escort vehicles are exposed to extreme anxiety, constant stress, and the daily trauma of deadly enemy action. This is exactly the type of mission that should be shared among units. We hear a great deal about their equipment wearing out from heavy use and the strain placed on supply lines, but little about the "wear and tear" on the people who operate this equipment. Korea and Vietnam are the only wars that I'm aware of where the U.S. military used a system of individual replacements, rather than rotating entire units. The lesson we learned with these wars was that sending men alone into units as fillers required more training and resulted in a feeling among soldiers that they were on their own, with little supervision, resulting in a breakdown of unit cohesion. The individual replacement system also resulted in more Battle Fatigue casualties, because soldiers lacked a support group of men and women with whom they had trained and would make the journey home.

6. **INTEGRATED SUPPORT ROLES:** It is a well-known fact that in Iraq and Afghanistan, the army and Marine Corps are suffering the largest number of casualties. In discussions with returning veterans of these wars, comments are often made about the shortage of forces available to fight and the limited participation of the navy and air force. This may seem strange to some, but these branches should not be denied the opportunity to participate in the ground war. Both of these components have many types of units that

could easily play a larger role in either a lead or support capacity, such as special operations, hospitals, medical personnel, security/police forces, helicopter, and small fixed wing pilots—the list goes on and on. The reason these "sister" forces are important is that, by using them, more Marines and soldiers could be released to fight the enemy. This would reduce the number of tours for everyone and, in the process, reduce the number of personnel exposed to Battle Fatigue. Current Defense Secretary Robert Gates has recently challenged the air force to contribute more to wartime needs, such as their unmanned surveillance aircraft and support crews.

7. **A TREATMENT THAT WORKS:** Despite the fact that PTSD has been around for centuries, health care professionals have had limited success in treating this condition. That is, until last year, when the military began using a treatment technique known as (Eye Movement Desensitization and Reprocessing (EMDR), which deals with stimulating the brain's right and left hemispheres through bilateral movement. Despite evidence documented in research and journal articles that EMDR works, some people still do not use the technique. The question is, "Why isn't it being used more?" This treatment is the best we have for helping people to recover from the psychological wounds of combat and move back to civilian life. Controlled studies clearly show sufficient results to judge EMDR as an effective treatment for PTSD. Active military treatment facilities and VA hospitals should immediately train their therapy staffs in the use of EMDR and pull out all the stops in funding this program. This is a technique that actually works, and treatment hospitals adopting its use could begin to see great increases in their success rates. (Individuals who want to take charge of their own treatment can find a qualified EMDR therapist in their area at http://emdria.org/.)

__CONCLUSION__

To wrap-up this discussion of Battle Fatigue, I offer these final words: It is our nation's great shame that we are benefiting from the sacrifices of so few American families and have given them so little in return. The government has been slow to respond to its military citizens' requests for assistance; equipment has not always been first-rate, and our outdated health care programs have burdened our injured with a bureaucracy that has delayed care and made recovery more difficult. Our countrymen have not lobbied policy makers enough to increase benefits for the armed forces or veterans. The majority of Americans are uninvolved; they have not rationed, bought war bonds, or paid more taxes to purchase the national security and freedom that are being paid for by the blood and sacrifice of our servicemen and women on distant battlefields. As the world's only superpower and its richest, we must do better. Our servicemen and women are the nation's most precious assets, and they deserve better educated leadership, higher pay, and greater benefits. Furthermore, above all else, if any of these young men or women should happen to come home wounded, then he or she must receive the finest medical care money can buy—particularly if that soldier is one of the "silent casualties among us."

Appendix A

Resource List

National Center for PTSD

The National Center for PTSD was created in 1989 by Congress to address the needs of veterans diagnosed with military-related PTSD. This Web site provides extensive information on trauma for clinicians, veterans, and their families.

www.ncptsd.va.gov

Veterans Center Readjustment Counseling Service (VETCENTERS)

These centers, staffed by veterans, are located throughout the country and provide a variety of services, including counseling to veterans and their families.

www.va.gov/res/index.htm

Ameriforce Deployment Guide

This guide provides valuable information on deployment for veterans and their families. The site was designed to improve online communication between deployed soldiers and their families.

www.armyfrg.org/skins/ArmyFRG/displays.aspx

American Academy of Sleep Medicine

This Web site provides information from the American Academy of Sleep Medicine on sleep medicine and related research. The AASM's mission is to assure quality care for patients with sleep disorders, promote the advancement of sleep research, and provide public and professional education.

www.sleepfoundation.org

USA National Suicide Hotlines

http://suicidehotlines.com

800-784-2433

800-273-8255

Military Order of the Purple Heart

This Web site assists wounded veterans in obtaining benefits and receiving treatment. Veterans do not need to have been awarded the Purple Heart to receive service.

703-354-2140

http://www.purpleheart.org

EMDR International Association

Web site for one of the leading treatment approaches for PTSD. A practitioner directory can be found at this site.

http://emdria.org/

Alcoholics Anonymous

This is the largest and most well-known international self-help organization for recovering alcoholics. You can locate meetings in your area by navigating this Web site.

www.alcoholics-anonymous.org

National Amputation Foundation

Founded in 1919, this association offers assistance such as peer counseling, support, and referral information to American war veterans who are amputees.

www.nationalamputation.org

Anxiety

This Web site claims to be the oldest Internet resource offering services and support for those who suffer from anxiety and panic attacks. It provides information about anxiety disorders and the various types of support available.

www.algy.com/anxiety/anxiety.php

Military OneSource

This organization provides various kinds of services, including counseling to active duty members and their families. Reservists and National Guard personnel, along with their families, can also use this organization if they're on active duty.

www.militaryonesource.com

Department of Veterans Affairs

This is the main Web site for the VA. Those eligible for benefits should begin their search here.

www.va.gov

Seamless Transition Homepage

This is the VA's Web site for veterans returning from Iraq and Afghanistan. You can locate a VA center near you by using this Web site.

www.seamlesstransition.va.gov

Traumatic Brain Injury

This organization provides advocacy, education, research, and prevention information on traumatic brain injury.

www.biausa.org/pages/home.html

Defense and Veterans Brain Injury Center

This program, administered jointly by both the Department of Defense and the Department of Veterans Affairs, has a mission to "serve veterans with traumatic brain injury and their dependents, through state-of-the-art medical care, innovative clinical research initiatives, and educational programs."

800-870-9244

www.dvbic.org

Appendix B

Stars and Stripes Articles

<u>Seeing Relief from Post-Traumatic Stress: Therapists Trained in Eye Movement Desensitization and Reprocessing at Landstuhl</u>

by Steve Mraz, Mideast edition,
Stars and Stripes, August 7, 2007

Landstuhl, Germany, Mental Health care providers are reporting positive results using a relatively new and nontraditional treatment for post-traumatic stress disorder at Landstuhl Regional Medical Center. During the past few weeks, about a dozen social workers, psychologists, and other mental health professionals at Landstuhl have been trained to perform a treatment called Eye Movement Desensitization and Reprocessing. Developed in the late 1980s by psychologist Francine Shapiro, eye movement desensitization and reprocessing, or EMDR, deals with stimulating the brain's right and left hemispheres through bilateral movement. That bilateral movement usually comes in the form of patients following a therapist's fingers back and forth with their eyes. With patients told to recall a painful memory while moving their eyes back and forth, EMDR may seem like some mumbo-jumbo, hypnotic cure. But the Department of Defense and the Department of Veterans Affairs strongly recommend EMDR as one of four treatments for PTSD in military and nonmilitary populations. The treatment is one of several standard therapies being used by counselors at Walter Reed Army Medical Center in Washington DC. The treatment, during which patients are fully awake and alert, produces positive results that can be demonstrated, said Dr. Hohn Hartung, a trainer with EMDR Institute who is conducting the training at Landstuhl with a colleague. "It's much more than moving your eyes while thinking of a disturbing thought," he said. Researchers cannot explain exactly how or why EMDR works, but it does work, they say. Brain scans of patients recalling a traumatic memory show a lopsided image, Hartung explained. The parts of the brain responsible for negative emotions and protecting us from danger in emergencies are highly active. The portions of the brain that control positive emotions, language, and common sense are basically shut down, Hartung said.

"You put that all together, and you've got a person under trauma overreacting to innocuous stimuli," he said. "Now here's the really good news. We can't tell you exactly how we get there, but we know where we get. Four and a half hours later with EMDR treatment, we take a picture of that person's brain. As the person thinks of that trauma now, it's no longer traumatic. The brain is flashing on both sides, nicely balanced." The 4½ hours comes from three 90-minute sessions typical with EMDR treatment. Despite evidence in research and journal articles that EMDR works, some people still do not use the technique, Hartung said. The question is, Why isn't it being used more?" He said, "This is the best we have for helping people recover from the wounds of combat and move back to civilian life."

Those interested in more information about this procedure should refer to the Resource List in Appendix A for the Web site or phone number of EMDR health care professionals in your area.

Military Aims to Remove Stigma from Seeking Therapy for Post-Combat Stress

by Nancy Montgomery. European edition,
Stars and Stripes, August 4, 2005

When Capt. John Trylch of the First Squadron, Fourth U.S. Cavalry Regiment made it safely back from Iraq, he expected things would be different, that he would be different.

"I kept waiting. Where's the change? Where's the change?" he said. "But you find yourself falling into the same routines. I was surprised by that."

Trylch is among the more than 80 percent of U.S. soldiers who, new studies are finding, served in battle in Iraq and came back home apparently unchanged, without a psychological problem, despite the stress and tragedy of war.

But he's well aware of the other 15 percent to 20 percent whose combat duty leaves them with psychological wounds—depression, anxiety, post-traumatic stress disorder among them—that the military is showing interest in trying to treat. Two of Trylch's soldiers had to be evacuated out of Iraq because of mental health problems, he said, and more returned from battle with symptoms of depression or anxiety that they hadn't had before.

He said he wanted to make sure they knew seeking help was the way to go.

A landmark 2004 study by researchers from the Walter Reed Army Institute of Research, thought to be one of the first to examine battle-related psychological problems of active duty soldiers, found that there was a significant barrier to troops seeking mental health care.

The barrier, according to the study of more than 6,100 soldiers and marines who'd deployed to Iraq and Afghanistan, was the belief that seeking counseling would harm military careers and stigmatize armed forces members as weak. Fifty percent of troops in that study showing symptoms of mental health problems said it would be bad for their career to see a counselor, 65 percent said they'd be perceived as weak, and 63 percent said commanders would treat them differently.

"We all read the study," said LTC. Christopher Kolenda, 1/4 Cavalry Commander. "We said, 'We've got to do better.'"

The 1/4 Cavalry, then under the command of LTC. Jim Chevallier and deployed near Samarra, Iraq, joined with chaplains and military psychologists to try to remove the stigma of seeking mental health care and to bring greater attention to the issue.

They invited the U.S. Army Medical Research Unit, Europe, based in Heidelberg, to do pre-deployment and post-deployment mental health screenings to aid in further research into the types of emotional changes soldiers undergo in combat and how to deal with them.

Additionally, services and information for family members in Germany were stepped up.

"If we got the families comfortable with the process, the more likely it was that they would encourage their soldier to get the help they needed," Kolenda said. "It doesn't mean you're weak; it doesn't mean you're going to be treated differently. It's all about assistance to overcome these wounds."

After the 1/4 Cavalry and Brigade Reconnaissance team returned to Schweinfurt, Germany, 732 of them filled out the mental-health screening forms. Of those, 135 (or 18.4 percent) were referred for follow-up psychological care.

But those soldiers also reported a much greater acceptance of mental health care. Just 9 percent of 1/4 Cavalry soldiers viewed counseling as detrimental to their careers, 14 percent said they'd be perceived as weak, and 17 percent said they thought their command would treat them differently.

"We worked really hard to break down these barriers," Kolenda said. But some portion of the barrier remains.

No 1/4V Cavalry soldiers undergoing counseling for post-combat psychological issues were willing to be interviewed about it, Trylch said.

The Heidelberg research unit still is working on its findings from the 1/4 Cavalry. One of the more intriguing questions being raised is whether it can be determined which of the many terrible things combat soldiers experience are most linked with post-traumatic stress syndrome. "Certain exposures that are so intense that they are hard-wired, almost , to produce post-traumatic stress," as LTC. Paul Bliese, research unit commander, puts it.

According to Trylch and two soldiers under his command, all who saw difficult duty, the absolute worst experience was easy to identify and very hard to forget: it was the deaths of three soldiers in their unit killed in action, among ten soldiers and one civilian the squadron lost in its year in Iraq.

Trylch credits his equanimity to the support of family and friends and to time spent thinking.

"Introspection—who I am and what I've seen and how I want to deal with that," Trylch said. "I've tried to reconcile them the best that I can, so that I can live with it.

"But do I look at the world through a little different set of eyes? Yeah, I do."

Special Team in Iraq Combats Stress, Not Insurgents

By Sandra Jontz, Mideast edition,
Stars and Stripes, April 30, 2005

BAGHDAD—To help troops deal with the mental strains of battle, members of the 55th Medical Company (Combat Stress Control) are trying to get closer to them.

Today, the soldier hoisting sandbags, working at a checkpoint, or assigned to a foot patrol could be a member of the stress control team, said Specialist Erik Gonzalez, 23, a mental health specialist assigned to Balad.

"We talk to the soldiers where they are. We go to them when they're standing guard, wherever they're working," said Gonzalez, from Chicago. "We're right out there with them, so they will talk to us."

"We want them to know that we're soldiers, too," said Staff Sgt. Thomas Hicks, 36, a medic and occupational therapist working out of Camp Cooke in Taji.

"If we walk a mile in your boots, we know what you go through. If we're sitting in a clinic all day, we're not getting anything done."

Members of the medical company say some soldiers, from the commanding echelons on down, still perceive asking for help with mental health problems as a sign of weakness. They say some leaders, at times, have shunned the aid offered by mental health professionals operating in combat fields.

"We go out there and tell commanding officers that we're actually a force multiplier, that we're here to increase the odds that they walk away from here with all their soldiers," said Hicks, from Muncie, Indiana.

In July 2003, the Army Surgeon General deployed a team to Iraq to study the mental health of troops following an increase in the number of suicides in the theater that month.

From August to October 2003, the twelve-member team of psychiatrists, psychologists, social workers, and personnel experts studied several areas of mental and behavioral health among the troops. Their recommendation included embedding combat stress teams with the troops on the front lines.

But a 2004 post-deployment screening conducted by the U.S. military showed that more than 50 percent of service members were reluctant to seek treatment for combat stress because they feared it would affect their careers or future promotions.

The military's approach today to mental health differs from that in past conflicts. Today, the philosophy is to get help to the front lines, so troops don't have to be separated from their units if a move to the rear is unnecessary. This way, troops aren't separated from their units, their friends, or their support, and they can get back to the job more quickly, said Maj. Heidi Ogden, 35, a psychiatrist working in Baghdad.

The combat stress teams, embedded with Army units throughout Iraq, work primarily a prevention mission, living the adage "an ounce of prevention is worth a pound of cure."

"We want to arm soldiers with skills to deal with stress, anger, frustration, loneliness, and other emotions that might prevent them from being their best on the job," Hicks said.

The presence of the mental health specialists is often greeted with laughter, sometimes nervous laughter, said Specialist Matthew Walerysiak, 22, an occupational therapist working in Baghdad.

Their services are available to all, from infantry and artillery to support personnel. Everyone in a combat zone experiences some degree of stress, they said.

"We've heard some say, 'I don't see combat, I don't need your help,'" Walerysiak said.

"You're still in a combat zone where people want you dead," Hicks tells them. "That's stressful."

"You've left your life to be here, and if you're in the National Guard or Reserve, you've left your normal life and your job to be a soldier. Soldiering is stressful."

Sometimes the stress isn't caused by being on the front, team members said. Soldiers' thoughts can be miles from the battlefield, focused on matters on the home front.

When prevention fails, or it's not taken advantage of, the short-term cure is the "restoration unit" in Baghdad. That is where troops go, usually for about seventy-two hours or more, depending on the care required for treatment that includes intensive stress management and an opportunity to relax, Ogden said.

"But that's the last resort. What we try to do is treat them at the front lines," she said.

Number of Veterans Seeking Treatment for Stress Has Doubled

by Leo Shane III, Mideast edition,
Stars and Stripes, edition on November 2, 2006

WASHINGTON—The number of Iraq and Afghanistan veterans getting treatment for post-traumatic stress disorder nearly doubled from fall 2005, to this summer, but officials from the Department of Veterans Affairs say that isn't necessarily bad news.

They believe the increase points to a growing awareness of the symptoms of PTSD and a larger willingness among young veterans to seek out help for the illness.

According to internal department data, the number of young veterans receiving PTSD treatment from VA hospitals and counseling centers rose from 20,394 patients in September 2005, to 38,144 patients in June 2006, an increase of 87 percent.

Hospital cases alone totaled 29,041 in June, up 82 percent from nine months earlier. The number of veterans who visited counseling centers more than doubled from 4,467 to 9,103 over that same period.

Dr. Ira Katz, VA deputy chief of patient mental health services, said at least some of that increase is due to the increasing number of veterans: The number of troops who have separated from the service since September 2002, grew to 588,923 this summer, up more than 150,000 from the previous year.

Inevitably, any increase in veterans means more patients for the VA hospitals, he said.

But Alfonso Batres, chief officer for the department's readjustment services, says he thinks most of the jump in the number of cases is directly related to outreach efforts over the last few years.

Overall, the number of Iraq and Afghanistan veterans visiting VA centers for any type of counseling rose from 43,682 in September 2005, to 144,227.

"We've really concentrated our efforts on reaching these troops," he said, "and now we're seeing more and more of them coming to the counseling centers."

The VA has been emphasizing stress disorders and their symptoms through public campaigns and information given to troops before they leave the military.

Batres said that, in addition, for the last two years, about 100 VA workers—all retired military personnel who served in Iraq and Afghanistan—have been stationed at demobilization sites overseas to talk about PTSD and veterans benefits for troops, to give them a better idea of what to expect after they leave the services.

"There is no one better to let (troops) know about that than their fellow peers," Batres said. "They're really getting the message out."

Batres also said the Defense Department's post-deployment mental health assessment, now repeated three to six months after troops return from combat tours overseas, has also greatly raised awareness of PTSD and its symptoms.

Both Katz and Batres said the department is working to add more counselors to its payroll to help deal with the increased workload, but they said the medical facilities are handling all of the current cases without significant problems.

Officer Sees "Perfect Storm" Brewing in Military's Mental Health Care System

by Allison Batdorff, Pacific edition,
Stars and Stripes, September 22, 2006

YOKOSUKA NAVAL BASE, JAPAN—Gaps in care, combined with the stress of combat in Iraq and Afghanistan are creating a "perfect storm" within the U.S. military mental health system according to a navy commander who spoke at Yokosuka Naval base on Wednesday.

Quick to say that his opinions are unofficial, the product of his twenty-four-year military career and not of the U.S. Navy or Department of Defense, Cmdr. Mark Russell gave a well-attended lecture called "Broken Promises: The Unspoken Truth of Mental Health Care in the DOD" during the final day of the Multinational Medical Conference. Russell, a child psychologist and director of education and development intervention services for bases across Japan, painted a picture of unmet needs and unrecognized opportunity stemming from the global war on terrorism.

"We are in a crisis situation," Russell said. "And it's going to get worse."

"We're making progress but are far from making good on our promise to provide the best mental health care possible for the men and women we send to war," Russell told the gathering.

More than fifty-six thousand troops, or 10 percent, have returned from Iraq and Afghanistan with a mental health diagnosis, making up a third of those in Veterans Affairs care. The cost of mental health care is high, he said. The VA spent $4.3 billion on post-traumatic stress disorder alone in 2004. Also, of the 9,145 (out of a possible 178,644) veterans who showed signs of PTSD between 2001 and 2004, only 22 percent were referred on to mental health care. That creates a chasm between a need for care and actually getting it, Russell said.

Another gap falls between DOD guidelines for mental health treatment and the training given to mental health workers, he said.

"Out of 133 mental health providers I surveyed, 90 percent of them had no training in the top four treatments the DOD recommends for PTSD," Russell said.

There also are problems with leadership, high burnout rates among caregivers, and the tendency to treat those suffering from hyperarousal compared to those who dissociate, he said.

"The bottom line is that we have increased demand and fewer resources to meet that demand," Russell said.

But the DOD has made significant strides, especially in terms of frontline combat mental health care, he added. The military's PIES system, basing combat mental health care on Proximity, Immediacy, Expectancy, and Simplicity, is working, he said.

"VThe numbers of mental health workers on the front lines is unprecedented," Russell said. "This is an all-out effort."

More troops are using frontline mental health services, with 40 percent getting help in 2005, compared to 29 percent in 2004. And, most importantly, 90 percent of those who get frontline help return to duty, he said.

The DOD also has improved screening programs, has established deployment centers with quality information, is conducting more surveys, and is getting more information out to veterans after they come home, Russell said.

"But the DOD could be doing more for the troops, caregivers, and for combat mental health in terms of treating the 'invisible wounds of warfare,'" he said.

"Right now, the DOD is in a historically unique position to lead the world in understanding, assessment, prevention, and treatment." Russell said. "Have we advanced science?"

The military has a "love/hate relationship" with mental health care, he added.

"We like it in war and know that increased mental health is a force multiplier," Russell said. "But in peacetime, mental health falls to the low end of the totem pole."

It's up to the military health professionals today to "take up the sword," he said.

"I've already turned in my retirement paperwork," he said.

Army Takes Aim at Post-Traumatic Stress

by Joseph Giordono, Pacific edition,
Stars and Stripes, June 18, 2004

YONGSAN GARRISON, SOUTH KOREA—With an increasing number of soldiers rotating to or from South Korea to combat zones and therefore more exposed to triggers of acute stress disorder or post-traumatic stress disorder, military medical officials here say they're focusing on both preventive and treatment programs.

Second Infantry Brigade soldiers deploying to Iraq later this summer, for example, already should be getting information on coping strategies and possible symptoms. Unit commanders and senior noncommissioned officers are the key link in getting information to soldiers, medical officials said, because military educational and treatment programs are in place.

The system focuses "not just on medical interventions but helping in terms of some of the social distress or other problems people are experiencing," said Maj. V Sheila Adams, the chief of social work at Yongsan Garrison's 121st General Hospital and the social work consultant to the 18th Medical Command. "It's really outlined in terms of trying to intervene and developing a comprehensive treatment plan."

Before units deploy, mental health experts in South Korea are meeting extensively with unit leaders to brief them on stress reactions in an effort to preempt any problems, Adams said. The leadership is given specific tips on both trying to prevent and, if necessary, to begin addressing problems.

Unique to South Korea, said Maj. Geoffrey Gabriel, the acting chief of psychiatry at the 121st General Hospital, is the ability and willingness of general medical officers at outlying camps to refer possible stress-related cases to experts at Yongsan.

The 121st also plans to hold a two-day summit of medical personnel in South Korea in coming weeks, specifically to address stress disorders. And the hospital plans to start a "stress management group" for soldiers and leaders at bases here.

"At least from the psychiatric standpoint, the army is really responding to this," Gabriel said.

Though by no means a new disorder, PTSD first was codified in the early 1980s and added to the *Diagnostic and Statistical Manual of Mental Disorders*, which the military used as its guide for mental health issues.

Persons exposed to life-threatening or shocking events can experience a range of symptoms, from mild temporary reactions to complex PTSD. Stress disorders have clear biological and psychological symptoms and very specific diagnoses, mental health professionals said.

According to the National Center for Post-traumatic Stress Disorder, "about 30 percent of the men and women who have spent time in war zones experience PTSD. An additional 20–25 percent have had partial PTSD at some point in their lives."

A national study of American civilians conducted in 1995 estimated that the lifetime prevalence of PTSD was 5 percent in men and 10 percent in women.

The numbers peaked with more than half of all male Vietnam veterans and almost half of all female Vietnam veterans having experienced "clinically serious stress reaction symptoms." Studies estimate the numbers at 8 percent of Gulf War veterans. Data is not yet available for the current Iraq conflict, officials said.

The center was founded in 1989 within the Veterans Administration (now called the Department of Veterans Affairs) in response to a Congressional mandate to address the needs of military veterans. The center works closely with scholars and clinicians from the National Institutes of Health, the Department of Defense, and academic researchers.

The center's site also includes "*The Iraq War Clinician Guide, 2nd Edition*," which details the different circumstances, military policies, and potential stressors being faced by soldiers now deployed.

That guide details post-battle debriefings under a system called PIES: Proximity-Immediacy-Expectancy-Simplicity.

"Early intervention is provided close to a solder's unit, as soon as possible," the clinician's guide says. "Soldiers are told that their experience is normal and they can expect to return to their unit shortly. They are also provided simple interventions to counteract 'fatigue' (e.g., 'three hots and a cot').

"The point here is that soldiers who experience severe war-zone stress reactions likely will have received some sort of special care. On the other hand, it is without question stigmatizing for soldiers to share fear and doubt and to reveal signs of reduced capacity. This is especially true in the modern, all-volunteer military, with many soldiers looking to enhance their careers."

Thus, the *Clinician's Guide* states, some veterans who don't exhibit signs of PTSD until later "will have suffered silently and may still feel a great need not to show vulnerability because of shame."

Medical officials of the 121st Hospital agree there are many things that can be done while on deployment to help counter development of stress-related disorders.

In addition to the "three hots and a cot," Adams and Gabriel said, things as simple as talking with other unit members or chaplains after an engagement could help. Again, they said, the willingness and cooperation of unit commanders and NCOs to acknowledge potential cases would be crucial in early detection and treatment.

Services Seek Better Ways to Help Troops With Psychological Strain

by Sandra Jontz, European edition,
Stars and Stripes on July 2, 2004

ARLINGTON, VA—Troops surveyed after serving in Iraq and Afghanistan have indicated that the stigma of seeking counseling would keep them from doing so, said the two authors of an army battle stress study.

"The most important findings are the barriers to care," said co-author Army Col. Charles Hoge, chief of psychiatry and behavioral science at the Walter Reed Army Institute of Research.

"Soldiers and marines with mental health (issues) don't receive help because of the stigma."

Such a stigma isn't anything new, acknowledged the other co-principal investigator, Lt. Col. Carl Castro.

"Are the findings surprising? Not really. We know, for example, that combat impacts soldiers. We know that from previous wars. We know there is a cultural barrier and a stigma to seeking treatment."

But for the first time, the study puts a number to the fact, he said.

"This allows us to quantify the problem, to characterize what we are trying to address. And now, when we implement new programs, policies, and procedures, we will have the numbers to assess whether they are working."

"The whole reason we're conducting the study is to address this issue. We know we're not perfect. The army is a learning organization. We know there is a culture of stigma to mental health, and we need to find out exactly what those barriers are and what we can do as an organization to reduce or eliminate them."

"The military services have several initiatives to counter perceived barriers, some related to the study and some started independently to address problems of post-traumatic stress disorder, depression, suicides, and other mental health concerns," Castro said.

"One of the things we're doing is we're using training and education, telling the soldiers what they might experience and what to expect on the battlefield," said Castro, who also was one of twelve mental health experts who visited Iraq and Kuwait last summer and fall.

Part of their task included investigating suicides in the field. Last year, there were twenty-six self-inflicted deaths in Iraq and Kuwait between April and December, with twenty-four in the army and two in the Marine Corps.

"Troops indicated that receiving pre-deployment education and training made them more likely to both seek out mental help and to comfort a fellow soldier," Castro said.

The Pentagon's health system also is boosting the number of mental health counselors and social workers at primary care facilities, embedding mental health providers on the battlefield so troops don't have to leave their units to get treatment, and conducting mandatory post-deployment health assessments, which include a mental health evaluation, though they are not anonymous.

"The DOD-wide program Military OneSource lets members receive six free and confidential sessions with a civilian provider off-post, and thus outside of the military system and a member's chain of command," Castro said.

"The programs are less than a year old, and officials have no research data on their use or effectiveness as of yet," he said.

"In order to keep the service confidential, participants are issued an identification number. Those needing more than the six sessions must be brought back into the military medical system," he said.

Web sites are service specific: www.armyonesource.com, www.navyonesource.com, www.airforceonesource.com, and www.mccsonesource.com.

Overseas, people can call the following numbers for information: In Europe, the number is 00-800-4648-1077.

In Japan, if using phone company ITJ, the number is 0041-800-46481077.

For IDC, the prefix is 0061; KDD, the prefix is 001; and NTT, the prefix is 0033.

In South Korea, the DSN number is (550-2769) or commercial 001-80046481077.

The Doctor Is In When Troops Need to Work Through the Consequences of War

By Terry Boyd, European edition,
Stars and Stripes, September 10, 2003

FALLUJAH, IRAQ—This is the Wild West. It always has been.

Iraqis say that even Saddam Hussein's methods of mass murder couldn't pacify the area around Fallujah and Ramadi, about an hour's drive west of Baghdad.

Now the unenviable mission of bringing the region under control falls to the Brave Rifles, the Second Squadron, Third Armored Cavalry Regiment, at a base called MEK.

Guerrillas in the sector have killed at least two U.S. soldiers and wounded a dozen since late August. So it would figure that if Dr. Michael Banton, an army lieutenant colonel, were going to be hanging around some place, it would be Fallujah.

Banton, a psychiatrist, leads the 113th Combat Stress Control company under the Heidelberg, Germany-based 30th Medical Brigade. It is one of four combat stress detachments of seven or eight people working across Iraq. Teams consist of officers who are psychiatrists, psychologists, and social workers, as well as enlisted mental health experts.

Banton describes himself as the modern version of Sidney Friedman, Sigmund Freud's empathetic acolyte in the M*A*S*H television series. Friedman was the congenial shrink who always showed up to talk to soldiers and doctors through the horror. Casual. Funny. Irreverent. Compassionate.

Banton is not much different. A tall, relaxed man, he has the air of a guy just hanging out. But he is a man with a mission.

His job is to help soldiers who have just lost a comrade in arms to recover from the hard times and make sure they are in shape to continue their mission. When he was at MEK in late August, the Third ACR had just had a suicide on top of the two soldiers killed.

"If I do my job here, I won't be seeing them five years from now in my office," said Banton, a reservist with a private practice in St. Louis.

Banton believes it is best to keep soldiers with their units and to get them back to their jobs as soon as possible. That's best for the soldier and unit manning, in his opinion. It is also a departure from how the army used to do things.

"During World War II, when the army lost one out of four soldiers to what was called 'Battle Fatigue,' soldiers were evacuated to the rear,"

Banton said. "But taking soldiers from their units decreases chances of recovery," he added.

Now, stress teams go to soldiers for "critical-event debriefings" from between twenty-four hours and seventy-two hours after an incident. Had this method been in place during World War II, Blanton believes the military could have returned 80 percent of battle stress victims to duty, as it does now.

While the army has had such teams for a decade, it keeps refining methods to match societal changes.

"The 'Dear John' e-mail, for example, is the modern curse for soldiers," Banton said. So combat stress teams use a broad spectrum of treatments, including relaxation techniques, anger management, problem solving, and working through home-front issues—they even use massage.

"What the teams don't practice is 'a touchy-feely' sort of therapy," Banton stressed. "We're not going to ask you if you want to sleep with your mother," he said.

"The idea is to 'normalize the event to some extent' for the soldiers who's just seen his buddy's leg shot off.

"War is an abnormal event, but we assure soldiers they're experiencing normal reactions, tears, anger, denial to violence and death," the doctor said.

Banton said the most important thing his team can do for soldiers is to listen.

Officials with the Third Armored Cavalry Regiment (ACR) declined to make available soldiers who had talked to combat stress teams, citing privacy and patient/doctor confidentiality concerns. But one officer who has sat in on the sessions describes them as effective, even essential.

"It's almost like a group therapy session," said Maj. Chris Kennedy, squadron operations officer. "Like an after-action report. I was surprised how willing people were to participate. They talked out freely, openly."

"Combat stress teams try to include everyone on an affected mission in the sessions, which are led by the psychiatrist," Kennedy said.

"Sessions go step by step, from getting soldiers to talk about what they saw, to discussing how it makes each feel, and finally to getting any help the soldiers need," he said.

Typically, soldiers go through distinct phases: denial, anger, and finally survivors' guilt, blaming themselves for a buddy's death or injury. It's common for soldiers to replay events over and over, asking themselves if they made a mistake, Kennedy and Banton said.

"I've watched soldiers go through all the symptoms," Kennedy said. "Not necessarily in that order. But before they were through, they went through each stage."

"I had a soldier say, 'What if I'd just moved my Bradley to the right? I'd have seen that guy,'" Banton said. "In his mind, his friend would still be alive. You have to talk them through it. Make them realize everyone did their best."

"After an incident, speed is of the essence," Kennedy added. "Though it takes about forty-eight hours for events to settle enough to talk about them, any longer and you've waited too long," he said.

"One session didn't happen until four days after an attack because the unit was moving," Kennedy said. "One soldier said, 'I wish we'd done this earlier. I had just started to be able to deal with it.'" It (the session) was basically digging it up. Meaning they go through it all over again.

Kennedy is a believer in the effectiveness of the immediate sessions.

"Despite his unit taking multiple hits, the 2nd squadron hasn't evacuated one soldier," he said.

"I would hazard to say they're lifesavers, especially in Fallujah where guerrillas attack the 2nd every single day."

Col. Paul D. Walker (Ret)

Sigonella Team Helped Cole Sailors Deal with Stress, Grief

by Anthony Burgos, European edition,
Stars and Stripes, November 1, 2000

NAVAL AIR STATION SIGONELLA, SICILY—Saving the USS Cole from sinking was the crew's first battle after a bomb ripped a forty-foot by forty-foot hole into the ship's hull. Saving the Cole's crew from the blast's echo and clearing smoke after the attack was the mission of the Special Intervention Response Team from the Naval Hospital in Sigonella, Sicily.

The October 12 explosion crippled the billion-dollar destroyer, killed seventeen sailors, and wounded thirty-nine. And while the wounded have returned to the States, the almost three hundred remaining sailors had their own battles to face, some aboard the ship, others inside their heads.

"Imagine being one of the victims of the Oklahoma City bombing and having to live in the destroyed building," said Lt. Silvetti, who is part of the eight-person team that deployed to Aden, Yemen, two days after the attack. "That's what conditions were like when we got there."

The SIRT team, comprised of personnel from different medical fields, has a straightforward mission regarding the Cole: counsel the traumatized service-members. According to Chief Petty Officer Don Posson, SIRT member sent to the USS Cole, that's why they got the call.

"We were invited (by the Navy's 5th Fleet Central command) to aid the sailors on the Cole because they were familiar with the work we did in the past," Posson said. A team from Sigonella was sent to Bahrain following the Gulf Air crash in late August to counsel Navy personnel involved in search-and-recovery operations.

Posson said that as soon as they arrived in Yemen, they had a lot of work to do: "Most of the injured had already been evacuated, and the medical staff from the ship and Bahrain had been working hard. So, we helped sailors that were going through the grief cycle."

While sailors worked long hours to keep the ship afloat, they also had to deal with the shock of the attack. Many were experiencing nightmares, sleeplessness, vomiting, and lack of appetite.

"Some of them were so traumatized that they wouldn't sleep on the inside of the ship," Silvetti said. "These were all normal reactions to such a tragic event."

According to Posson, the team split up by rank to work with sailors at different levels.

"Our enlisted team members spoke with leading petty officers. The chiefs had one of their own to talk to, the same with officers," Posson said. "That way, we broke it down to smaller departments and were able to support the sailors more directly."

By talking to sailors before and after their work shifts, the team would assess how things were going. "It was hard because we are outsiders. But we would ask people to speak about what they were going through and to look out for each other," Silvetti said.

"Once the sailors realized that they were all experiencing the same stress-related illnesses, they took less time to recuperate and get back to the mission of saving their ship," Silvetti said.

Although most people take days or longer to rebound, the team had to make sure the process was accelerated, Silvetti said. Some sailors were prescribed sleeping medication. Others were coached on ways to combat stress and fatigue. "We told them to get sleep, no matter what time of day," he added.

Lieutenant Joe Taylor, another SIRT member, said the crew's resiliency pulled them through the traumatic times.

"They took a hit and still came back to save the ship," he said. "Their comradery will always stand out in my mind."

The vast majority of people who live through a life-changing event will be able to handle the stress that follows. But not everyone is so lucky.

"Statistically, 80 percent of people who go through a trauma of this type recover completely," Silvetti said. "It was the other 20 percent we had to help manage the stress. By the time we left, they were good to go."

As a matter of fact, Silvetti said that the Cole's career counselor said the crew's attitude toward the ship and the Navy may have changed after the fatal assault.

"Prior to the explosion, there weren't many sailors re-enlisting." Silvetti said. "But while we were there, we saw three re-enlistment ceremonies, and we were told that thirteen others were scheduled. They were proud of being members of the USS Cole team."

After eleven days in Yemen aboard the Cole, seven of Sigonella's counseling team went back to work at the base hospital Monday. Lieutenant Commander John Kennedy remained with the crew members in Yemen. According to a spokesperson from the Navy's 5th Fleet command in Bahrain, the remaining USS Cole crewmembers are to be flown back to Norfolk, Virginia, the ship's home port, but no time table has been announced yet.

The USS Cole was towed from the Aden on Sunday and is in the process of loading onto a Norwegian heavy-lift ship, the Blue Marlin. A group of sailors, engineers, and security personnel will travel on the Blue Marlin during its five-week trip to the United States.

Soldiers Need Tougher Psychological Emotional Training, Says Infantry Head

European edition,
Stars and Stripes, June 15, 2002

Today's soldier needs tougher psychological and emotional training for battle, the army's chief of infantry said at the annual Infantry Conference in Atlanta on Tuesday, the *Atlanta Journal and Constitution* reported.

Major General Paul Eaton said, "The army does a good job of preparing soldiers physically but dedicates the least amount of time to psychological and emotional readiness," according to the report.

"Infantry soldiers should receive rigorous training, similar to what Army Rangers go through, that tests their ability to withstand stress while also testing their judgment, values, confidences, and perseverance," Eaton said.

Such training would be expensive, Eaton was reported as saying. A possible model for such training is available from the Army Ranger School.

As an example of the psychological challenges young soldiers face, Eaton noted the dual roles of diplomat carrying out national policy and soldier ready to respond to attack, that troops sent on peacekeeping missions must play, the paper reported.

Military Health Officials Trying to Keep Pace with War's Mental Toll: Alcoholism Common for Those Afflicted with PTSD

By Matt Millham, V European edition,
Stars and Stripes, July 16, 2006

As an army computer specialist, Brian didn't expect to find himself in combat in Iraq. But two months after arriving in Baghdad, while on patrol with a cavalry unit, he faced his first of many brushes with death when a makeshift bomb exploded near his vehicle.

"That scared the (expletive) out of me," said Brian, which is not his real name. As a member of Alcoholics Anonymous who recently completed mandatory treatment for alcohol and drug abuse problems, he spoke on condition he wouldn't have to give his name.

Brian didn't realize his clashes on the battlefield had mentally scarred him, but memories of what he went through put him in a state of perpetual anxiety. After returning from Iraq, he dealt with his anxiety the same way many Vietnam veterans did and still do: He turned to alcohol and drugs.

Substance abuse often goes hand-in-hand with post-traumatic stress disorder, a psychiatric condition that affects roughly 15 percent of Vietnam veterans and perhaps as much as 17 percent of Iraq veterans, doctors say. The condition often occurs after experiencing or witnessing life-threatening events.

Soon after the war in Iraq started, the Department of Defense began screening returning combat vets for evidence of mental health issues so troubled troops could get help as soon as possible. The army also sent mental health professionals downrange to check on the quality of care troops were getting. The hope is that these efforts will keep new vets from suffering the mental health and substance abuse problems that plague Vietnam vets. If they fail, the result could look a lot like Brian did before treatment.

Having slipped through the PTSD screening process, Brian dulled his anxiety with a self-prescribed regimen of alcohol and drugs. His heavy drinking and risky behavior got him two charges of drunken driving in less than seven months.

"It wasn't until I got my second DWI that I was ready to admit I had a problem," he said.

He was about to get promoted to sergeant but instead was busted down to private, sentenced to forty-five days of extra duty and restriction, and had to forfeit pay. He was also ordered into the army substance abuse program.

It was only after his mental health had thrown his career on the rocks that doctors said he likely suffered from PTSD.

After the diagnosis, he was enrolled in a six-week, inpatient treatment program at Landstuhl Regional Medical Center in Landstuhl, Germany, that helped him deal with his dependence on alcohol and drugs and identify the events that had driven him to substance abuse.

"They did a great job with getting me the help I needed," Brian said.

If substance abuse among Iraq vets with PTSD follows the course of Vietnam vets, more than 13 percent of troops retuning from Iraq with mental health issues could be expected to find themselves in Brian's shoes, as they face alcohol or other substance abuse problems.

"I think a lot of that information is still coming in, "Kate Azar, the clinical director of Darmstadt, Germany's army substance abuse program, said. "That is something we are definitely keeping an eye on."

The DOD's efforts to rein in mental health problems among combat vets, though robust compared with those from any previous U.S. armed conflict, aren't going far enough for some.

In May, the Government Accountability Office filed a report that said only one out of every five troops who screened positive for PTSD upon leaving a war zone was referred for follow-up evaluations. But those in the military have been more optimistic about the mitigating effects of the mental health care now afforded troops.

A January 2005 report chartered by the U.S. Army Surgeon General said mental health and well-being improved from the first to the second year of the Iraq war. The report included troops stationed throughout the Middle East, including those in noncombat roles in places such as Kuwait and Qatar.

According to the report, 18 percent of troops screened positive for mental health issues during the first year of the war in Iraq. The number dropped to 13 percent among those who served during the second year of the war.

The army has continued to monitor troops' health, and, in November, a mental health advisory team finished looking at troops in the third Iraq rotation. What the team concludes might provide some insight into what happens when troops are sent back into the fray.

"The world is speculating that PTSD will be higher among troops who have been to Iraq more than once," said Col. Elspeth Ritchie, a psychiatry consultant to the Army Surgeon General.

Reports from two previous teams were filed within two to three months of their return from the field. "It has been eight months since the last team returned, and it has yet to file a report," Ritchie said. "The information isn't in yet; there's a lag time," Ritchie said.

If mental health issues among vets of Iraq and Afghanistan are on the rise, programs such as the army substance abuse program could soon find themselves overwhelmed.

Among Vietnam veterans seeking treatment for PTSD, 60–80 percent have alcohol use disorders, according to a fact sheet from the U.S. Department of Veterans Affairs' National Center for PTSD.

Robert McCollum, who runs the army substance abuse program for the Installation Management Agency-Europe, said the program's offices across the continent are already feeling the pressure. "My people are busy. Their plates are full, he said.

Troop's Health Woes Run Gamut from "Saddam's Revenge" V To Severe Stress

by Marni McEntee, European edition,
Stars and Stripes, October 29, 2003

BAGHDAD, IRAQ—In Iraq's harsh environment, even soldiers safe inside their base camp face dangers.

Between combat casualties and accident victims in Iraq, medical personnel are also busy fighting microscopic enemies that can lay a troop nearly as low as a gunshot wound.

With ailments ranging from "Saddam's revenge" stomach bugs to infections caused by bad hygiene, hundreds of soldiers are lining up at sick call instead of patrolling front lines.

"Some maladies are caused by a witch's brew of dust, heat, exotic bacteria, and vermin. Others stem from poor sanitation and close living quarters," said Capt. Jolene Lea, a community health nurse at the 28th Combat Support Hospital in Baghdad.

"Still others are related to the stress of seeing a friend killed in battle or hearing bad news from home," Lea said. Those can manifest themselves into mental health problems and sometimes, suicide.

"The most serious illness and injury cases are evacuated from Iraq to Landstuhl Regional Medical Center in Germany. As of last week, Landstuhl doctors have treated 7,381 from Operation Iraqi Freedom," hospital spokeswoman Marie Shaw said. "Only 10 percent of those casualties were from battle injuries," she said.

The problems have some troops at bases from Basra in the south to Mosul in the north afraid that living and working in Iraq may be bad for their health.

"I am very worried about the long-term health effects of this environment." Sergeant Brian Rau of the 372nd Military Police Company, in Hillah, wrote on a Stars and Stripes survey form. Stripes reporters surveyed nearly two thousand troops throughout the country in August.

"The food is bad and not reliable, so we eat on the local market every day," Rau wrote. "There is standing sewage outside our building. And the cans we use for toilets are prefilled with diesel fuel so we sit on top of those fumes daily."

Corporal Joshua Enos, a UH-60 Black Hawk crew chief who lived at an old Iraqi fighter base west of Qariya, worried about the effects of a massive fire that broke out in a nearby sulfur plant shortly after the 101stst Airborne Division took over the base in April. The fire spewed noxious black smoke into the air for days.

"Just walking out to the Humvee, I thought I was going to hyperventilate and die," Enos said. "It got so bad we were putting on our protective masks for a while. I don't even want to know what the long-term health effects of that are going to be."

Before deploying to the Middle East, most troops were briefed on the types of health issues they would face, Lea said.

Some conditions, such as an outbreak of pneumonia, were unexpected.

In all, ninety-eight troops from Iraq were diagnosed with pneumonia and nineteen became so ill they had to be placed on a ventilator and evacuated, said Virginia Stephanakis, a spokeswoman for the Army Surgeon General's Office. Two soldiers died.

Lea and other medical personnel from troop clinics to battalion aid stations, however, say the incidence of serious illness or injury in Iraq is proportionate to the population size.

"It's not like we're coming here and seeing things we don't see at home," said Maj. Bill Dixon, a physician at the 28th CHS. "I think the soldiers are holding up pretty well," Dixon said.

The following is a sample of the more common health problems in Iraq treated by military doctors at the 28th Combat Support Hospital during its first deployment 2003/2004:

eye injuries. Dust and windblown debris are the main culprits of eye abrasions. Doctors also have treated troops who have viral conjunctivitis.

fevers. Caused by inhalation of barnyard dust contaminated by a bacteria found in herd animals such as sheep and goats. Illness causes fever, sore throat, chills, nausea, vomiting, diarrhea, and chest pain.

gastrointestinal problems. Caused by tainted food or water. In June 2006, doctors treated a number of cases of Norwalk virus, a contagious stomach flu caused by ingesting food or water contaminated with fecal matter.

gynecology. Poor hygiene, stress, and other factors can cause female soldiers' menstrual cycles to stop or can cause infections. Several females also have been treated for breast masses.

heat injuries. Caused by dehydration, electrolyte abnormalities, and low sodium and potassium levels. At lease one soldier in Iraq has died from heatstroke.

kidney stones.: Caused by the inability to metabolize certain minerals in the bloodstream. Doctors at Landstuhl Regional Medical Center in Germany said cases may be caused by soldiers not drinking enough water or by drinking water with high-mineral content.

leishmaniasis. Caused by the bite from a parasite-infected sand fly. Serious cases need to be treated by a long course of antibiotics. Walter Reed Army Medical Center in Washington DC has treated twenty-two cases and the Armed Services Blood Program office has deferred troops returning from Iraq from donating blood for one year because of the problem.

orthopedic injuries. Including hernias, sprained ankles, and broken bones.

psychiatric problems. Ranging from Battle Fatigue to "adjustment disorders," to trouble adjusting to a new environment, to more serious mental health issues that lead to suicide. The Army is investigating eleven incidents of possible suicides and several other unexplained deaths.

respiratory illnesses. Dust, cigarette smoking, and pollution have contributed to an increase in asthma and bronchitis. At least ninety-eight soldiers have been diagnosed with pneumonia, and two soldiers have died from the condition.

swollen lymph nodes. Sometimes caused by an infected insect bite or other infections.

tuberculosis exposure. The illness is most common among enemy prisoners of war, but some soldiers have been exposed. Soldiers are routinely tested for tuberculosis exposure following deployments.

urology. Testicular masses and epididymitis, or an infection of the entrance to the urethra, caused by poor hygiene such as not changing underwear or showering regularly.

Appendix C

Symptoms of Traumatic Stress/Battle Fatigue

anger. Anger is a powerful emotion and is experienced for many reasons. Anger may be expressed with physical and emotional agitation, frustration, indignation, exasperation, hostility, or extreme displeasure. Anger can be expressed physically or emotionally toward oneself or others. Anger can be used as a distraction from sadness and helplessness, and sometimes in a relationship, couples fight to avoid sadness.

anxiety/hyperarousal. Anxiety is the normal alarm system alerting us to danger. Anxiety provides energy to get things done, to move through the day productively, and to keep safe. Sometimes anxiety gets out of control. A sense of dread or fear creeps over you. This may lead to generalized anxiety, in which you experience excessive worries or intense fears. Anxiety or hyperarousal of the senses can be a personal "alarm bell" that will not shut itself off. This internal perception of an alarm may grow as you experience excessive worries or fears intensely. Anxiety or hyper-arousal can be a personal "alarm bell" that doesn't shut off. This general anxiety may or may not be related to the initial experience that triggered it. Anxiety is not knowing what is coming next, or knowing, yet feeling helpless to change it.

chronic pain. Chronic pain lasts longer than six months. Sometimes the cause is unknown. Chronic pain is frustrating and can lead to depression, low self-esteem, and feelings of anger. Pain interferes with daily activity and relationships when the veteran becomes moody or irritable. Life can be disrupted by chronic pain. Response to pain varies with each person, depending on the location of the injury, how the injury occurred, pain threshold, personality, or a combination of stressors and a diagnosis of other injuries. Not all pain is due to injury. The meaning of illness or disability, according to the veterans' culture and benefits received, will also play a part in adjustment and acceptance of chronic pain.

compulsion. Behaviors that are repeated in an effort to avoid fear and anxiety caused by obsessions may become compulsions. Compulsive behavior is specific according to rules and rituals set by the individual. Common compulsions include chronic hand washing, cleaning the same room or object repeatedly, overgrooming, or repeating a song or word uncontrollably. Some sufferers "check" objects such as door locks or appliances to see if they are turned off, or drawers to be sure they are shut, or they turn a light on and off. Ordering excessively from home shopping television, collecting items, saving something, needing constant approval, or making phone calls may all become compulsions. You may be able to think of something personal that nearly became a compulsion in your life but you were able to get help or stop on your own. Compulsions may distract you from working on more painful issues.

confusion. Confusion is a condition of inattentiveness and memory difficulties. Confusion can lead to disruptive behavior, difficulty performing daily living skills, and isolation from family and friends. The veteran may lack awareness of his or her own position in time and space. She or he does not understand the here and now and cannot focus well enough to communicate effectively.

crisis. Crisis is an internal and external response that may occur following a stressful event that is perceived as a threat to the individual. A crisis response may be painful, as powerful emotions are experienced. An unexpected death may move one to a point of crisis. Living through a battle, life as a prisoner, life on a base in the States or abroad, or life on a ship or submarine would suggest some daily crisis of various magnitudes. You have probably lived through a "crisis." Some crisis responses are more difficult to overcome than others. Your individual response to crisis is unique to you and reflects your training to meet life's challenges, or the lack of it.

delusions. Delusions are fixed beliefs one may experience with some basis in reality. Delusional thinking may lead to feelings of anxiety and paranoia because of a loss of touch with reality. It is common for those experiencing delusions to deny they are experiencing them. The veteran may feel confused and unsafe if the delusions are frightening. Delusions may seem completely real. The veteran may believe he is back in combat. The family's response to someone experiencing delusions is often one of fear, depending on the severity of the delusion and the supports in place with which to cope. Education is important for the veteran and family, so everyone will understand delusional thinking.

denial. Denial is the refusal to acknowledge the truth about something. Denial is a defense mechanism used to protect against anxiety or emotional pain. You may be using denial unconsciously to avoid dealing with painful memories. Denial is a coping skill to protect you from stress, but it can backfire and make you feel worse. Veterans may try to convince themselves that everything is fine and that they do not need help. The truth may be that their lives are in chaos, and they are having a difficult time functioning. Often, veterans have difficulty accepting reality because it may imply vulnerability. The memories are sharp, and loyalties to those around them are fleeting. The veteran may feel out of control and terrified. Sometimes denial feels safer than reality.

dependence. Dependence is relying on someone else too much for constant support or aid. This can lead to an unhealthy need for physical contact, attention, help, approval, or repeated praise from others. Dependency issues can cause difficulty and confusion in one's life due to resistance to treatment, which is common. Veterans who are overly dependent may resist caring for themselves, feel helpless, cling to others, express physical complaints, demand extreme care, and become angry patients in the inpatient setting.

depression. Depression is a common symptom for those who have experienced trauma. It colors the way you feel, your attitude, and your beliefs about the world. Depression can look like sadness, or the veteran may cover his or her depression by smiling, making it difficult to detect. You will be sad when someone close to you dies, but clinical depression can last longer than ordinary grief. Depression looks different in everyone but produces some common symptoms. Signs of depression may include moving more slowly than normal, agitation, anxiety, fears, feelings of guilt, helplessness, frequent crying, withdrawal, difficulty making decisions, low self-esteem, a negative view of the world, substance abuse, or thoughts of suicide. Suicide is a leading cause of death and must be taken very seriously. Have a safety plan ready with a friend's number to call or get to a local emergency room if you ever are feeling suicidal.

disordered eating. Poor eating habits may result in a wide variety of physical or emotional concerns. Whatever the cause of poor eating, regaining healthy diet and exercise habits when recovering from trauma is helpful to the success of your recovery. Living with unhealthy eating habits affects many veterans significantly. Some seem to adjust well to the extra weight, but most run the risk of serious physical complications such as diabetes, heart disease, stroke, high cholesterol, osteoporosis, or skeletal problems. Emotional difficulties such as anger, anxiety, depression, low self-esteem, guilt, or frustration are frequently experienced by the veteran with an eating disorder.

flashbacks. A flashback is a timeless moment taking one back to where no one wants to go. The body remembers what occurred, and the brain is a powerful organ that remembers these incidents. The flashback represents unfinished business, a choice that has unacceptable results, or an attempt to master something you cannot control or handle. The individual having this symptom may be unaware of triggers to flashbacks such as the noise of a helicopter flying overhead, a loud bang nearby, a smell of a dead animal, a color, or the sound of a foreign language—all of which can lead to suddenly finding oneself in another place, mentally, emotionally, and even physiologically. The lack of control and not being able to trust your body, shattered assumptions, and everything that has been trusted is suddenly gone. The body is paralyzed in a frozen state. This is a dangerous way to live because you can be "called away" to a different place at any time. You may hear the term "dissociate," which is to be in one place physically but not mentally present when you are an involuntary witness to your traumatic past. Flashbacks do not have to control your life; you must take back control. It is crucial to discover what triggers flashbacks and disruptive moments. These lapses must be filled with healthy emotions, living in the present, and leading a normal life.

grief. Grief is a normal, healthy response when you have experienced a loss in your life. Everyone has a personal response to loss, and no response is wrong. Some recover quickly, and some feel symptoms of grief for a very long time. The healing process seems easier to bear with support. Rituals are a healing part of all cultures and vary among nationalities within our country. The funeral ceremony is a useful societal tool for grief and loss. In training exercises and combat, there may not be adequate time to stop for the grief process to run its course. Symptoms of shock, anger, pain, sadness, guilt, and denial become buried within the veteran/soldier. You may be able to discuss with your counselor losses that have been within your memory for a long time and feel unresolved. Remembering them and talking about them may begin the healing process.

guilt. Guilt is a strong feeling of remorse that results from feeling you have done something wrong. The veteran may have carried guilt for many years from service-related experiences. "Survivor's guilt" is common among accident victims and veterans who have survived when fellow soldiers have suffered or died. Feelings that accompany guilt may be shame, disgrace, embarrassment, regret, insecurity, anxiety, low self-esteem, or anger. Guilt colors the way a veteran sees himself or herself and the world. You relate to your family differently now, and your job performance may be affected. You may find it difficult to be "yourself" in social situations, where before you enjoyed a normal social life. Isolation is marked by withdrawn behaviors, avoidance, and silence. Isolated individuals may have poor ability to relate to others, and relationships may break down. Veterans may be preoccupied with memories of their service experiences and lost allies and may have difficulties sharing thoughts about anger, sadness, guilt, or other feelings. These service member want to be alone and eventually shut themselves off completely. They may begin to avoid and isolate themselves from those who offer support. Avoidance is one of the key symptoms of the diagnosis of PTSD.

loneliness. Loneliness is a feeling of lack of intimacy on many levels. Often, there is a profound feeling of a lack of contact, an "aloneness," where there is no one to whom the sufferer can turn in his solitude. Lack of intimacy may lead to emotional isolation, which may lead to social isolation. This symptom of trauma is one of the most common. As a result of ongoing loneliness, the individual may also notice symptoms of depression, anxiety, and various physical illnesses.

low self-esteem. Negative self-concept is the belief that you are just not quite good enough. Your identity is not as positive as it might be, for any number of reasons. You question your abilities, capabilities, worth, intelligence, or appearance. The future is not looking positive to you because your view of yourself isn't, perhaps, as others see you. You refuse to "give yourself a break." Low self-esteem can be the result of a negative self-image. Low self-esteem may lead to feelings of inferiority, failure, incompetence, and inadequacy, Veterans may become tired of these feelings and frustrated to the point of thinking of ending their lives. Whatever the cause of these suicidal thoughts, it is important to seek support immediately for you and your loved ones in such a position.

obsessions. Obsessions are persistent and recurring thoughts, ideas, impulses, images, or urges that permeate consciousness. Obsessions become involuntary and seem to have a life of their own. Obsessions become central to the thought process. Obsessions vary in their intensity; therefore, veterans who suffer from obsessions can be disturbed by them to varying degrees. Treatment takes time and patience. There is a reason you are thinking this way, and your health care provider can offer help, encouragement, and support.

paranoia/hypervigilance. Paranoia is a haunting feeling of mistrust. Paranoia, a medical term that is used to describe an ongoing feeling that someone is after you, may also involve other intrusive thoughts. Paranoia can interfere with every aspect of your life, as you fear intimacy and isolate yourself. The veteran may move away from family, friends, and all support, in an effort to feel safe because of suspicions and paranoid feelings. In fact, being alone can increase feelings of paranoia. The anxiety, depression, and other aftereffects of trauma require support and understanding. Without intervention, fear from memories and trauma of the past will only continue to haunt the veteran. The Hypervigilance part of this condition is a form of high alert where you are constantly on the lookout for threats in your environment. This level of alert is a survival skill learned in stressful situations that may result in the veteran "constantly checking the perimeter" or needing to sit with his back to the wall, so that nothing sneaks up on him or the need to be armed. Hypervigilance sometimes peaks as a startle reaction.

passive-aggressive behavior. Passive-aggressive behavior is a dysfunctional form of communication that sends mixed signals. It is an indirect way of communication in which the veteran expresses anger and hostility and is a provocative way of communicating. The individual's unpredictability usually makes others fear him or her. This behavior can create serious conflicts with others, which could lead to frustration in relationships and emotional as well as physical violence. The most frequent outcome of this condition is divorce and job loss.

phobia. A phobia is an irrational thought that is often frightening, about a specific object, activity, or situation. Phobias vary in intensity. Some are common and annoying but tolerable. Others are dysfunctional and interfere with the veteran and his family's life, to varying degrees. A phobia can become so intense that the sufferer cannot leave his home for fear of coming into contact with the object he fears. Common phobias include fear of snakes, mice, or spiders. Phobias associated with veterans include fear of guns, crowded places, sudden movements, loud noises, or screams. A phobia interferes with your social and personal life, and without treatment, the fear intensifies. The veteran may feel he is going crazy or losing control. Phobias may also lead to isolation and feelings of paranoia.

secondary traumatic stress disorder. Those who, in some way, have been associated with individuals who suffer from trauma may also become traumatized and experience what is called secondary traumatic stress disorder. Traumatic experiences and combat-related active duty may break down family relationships of the veteran. It is possible that those in the veteran's life may begin to exhibit characteristics or symptoms similar to post-traumatic stress. Even the children of combat veterans sometimes are diagnosed with PTSD. These children exhibit impaired self-esteem, hyperactivity, poor reality testing, and aggressive behavior. They may also have difficulty coping with guilt, and may feel fear, rage, mistrust.

sexual trauma. Sexual trauma is when sexual intercourse has occurred against the victim's will, and the victim has not emotionally recovered. The trauma has remained. It is listed among the symptoms of post-traumatic stress because of the number of veterans who have experienced sexual assault. When this has occurred, the experience may or may not have been reported. The veteran may or may not have received medical or psychiatric treatment. Rape usually includes use of force, threat, intimidation, or lack of consent of the victim, who can be either male or female. Recovery from sexual trauma is a difficult and painful process. Without support and psychotherapy, either individual or in a group, it is possible the symptoms will worsen and may include mood instability, flashbacks, and memories of the event. It may be very difficult to learn to trust anyone after such an event as rape. You may have very few close relationships and may unknowingly sabotage the relationships you manage to form. You may develop a fear of intimacy, sexual experiences may take on a frightening dimension, or you may become promiscuous. You may also become confused and frustrated.

sleep disorders. When you are diagnosed with a sleep disorder, you either sleep too much, which is called hypersomnia, or you have difficulty falling asleep and staying asleep, which is called insomnia. A confirmed diagnosis of PTSD almost certainly means you will have sleep disturbances of some sort. It is very important, for a complete recovery, to find out why you are not sleeping soundly. Most adults benefit from about eight hours of sleep every night and lack energy when they go to bed too late or stay in bed too long. In veterans, sleep disturbance may be triggered by having seen a violent movie or news footage of a battle. Sleep disorders have both physical and emotional symptoms, which may include racing thoughts, nightmares, rapid heart rate, night sweats, headache, nausea, or other symptoms of anxiety, as you struggle to sleep or find yourself unable to sleep. Disordered sleep can begin and gather steam secondary to any of the other post-trauma symptoms.

substance abuse. Substance abuse is the excessive use of alcohol, various substances, and prescription drugs. The substance of abuse may be food, marijuana, caffeine, or nicotine. Substance abuse, usually an attempt by the soldier or veteran to self-medicate, often leads to addiction. Addiction requires treatment for recovery to occur and be sustained. There are many choices for treatment; the key again is diagnosis, education, support, and treatment.

suicidal thoughts. When a veteran is experiencing depression, deep sadness, or perhaps psychosis, there may be a point when he begins to think about ending his life. As these thoughts begin to formulate and take shape, they may become repetitive. Thoughts range from the vague hopelessness of wanting to go away in order to be alone, to sleeping forever, to just wanting to die. Suicidal thoughts must be taken seriously the first time and treated immediately. Prescription medication may be very helpful in treating the mood that most often precipitates suicidal thoughts.

Bibliography

Ambrose, Stephen E. *Americans at War*. New York: Berkley Books, 1997.

American Psychiatric Association. *Diagnostic and Statistical Manual of Mental Disorders*. 4th ed. Washington DC: American Psychiatric Association, 2000.

American Psychiatric Association. *Quick Reference to the Diagnostic Criteria from* DSM-IV-TR. Washington DC: The American Psychiatric Association, 2000.

Armstrong, Keith, Suzanne Best, and Paula Domenici. *Courage after Fire*. Ulysses Press, 2006.

Bayley, Alan. "Brain Trauma: A Toll of War." *Kansas City Star*, January 13, 2008.

Beasley, W. G. *The Japanese Experience*. Berkeley: University of California Press, 1999.

Beckham, J., S. Moore, M. Feldman, M. Hertzberg, A. Kirby, and J. Fairbank. "Health Status, Symptoms, and Severity of Post-traumatic Stress Disorder in Vietnam Combat Veterans with Post-traumatic Stress Disorder." *American Journal of Psychiatry* (1998).

The Boston Globe, "Soldiers Face Neglect at Medical Facility," February 19, 2007.

Bradley, James. *Flags of Our Fathers*. New York: Bantam Books, 2000.

CinCHouse.com. "Backing in to PTSD: PTSD's Physical Impact." (April 1, 2008) http://cinchouse.com/article.asp?.

Copeland, Mary Ellen. *The Depression Workbook: A Guide for Living with Depression and Manic Depression*. New Harbinger Publications, 2002.

Deseret Morning News. "Repeated Deployments Called Serious Mental Health Risk," May 4, 2007.

Erickson, D., J. Wolfe, L. King, and E. Sharkansky. "Post-traumatic Stress Disorder and Depression Comparisons in a Sample of Gulf War Veterans: A Prospective Analysis." *Journal of Consulting and Clinical Psychology* 69 (2001): 41–49.

Figley, C. R., ed. *Compassion Fatigue: Coping with Secondary Traumatic Stress Disorder in Those Who Treat the Traumatized.* NT: Brunner/Mazel, 1995.

Fisher, R. *The Knight in Rusty Armor.* Melvin Powers Wilshire Book Company, 1989.

Ford, J. "Disorders of Extreme Stress Following War-Zone Military Trauma: Associated Features of Post-Traumatic Stress Disorder or Comorbid But Distinct Syndromes." *Journal of Consulting and Clinical Psychology* 67 (1999): 3–12.

Gordon, Suzanne. *Nursing against the Odds.* Cornell University Press, 2006.

Gottfried, Jean-Louis. *The Mild Traumatic Brain Injury Workbook: Your Program for Regaining Cognitive Function and Overcoming Emotional Pain.* New Harbinger Publications, 2004.

Gronwall, D. M. A., Philip Wrightson, and Peter Waddell. *Head Injury: The Facts: A Guide for Families and Caregivers.* Oxford Medical Publications, 1998.

Lanham, Stephanie. *Veterans and Families' Guide to Recovering from PTSD*, (4th edition). Stephanie Laite Lanham, 2007.

Manchester, William. *American Caesar.* Boston: Little, Brown and Co., 1978.

Mental Health Advisory Team V Report. *Operation Iraqi Freedom 06-08.* February 14, 2008. Office of the Surgeon, Multi-National Force-Iraq.

Military.Com. "Army Expands PTSD Screening Program." (April 11, 2008) http://www.military.com/military-report/army.

National Center for PTSD. "Alcohol Problems Often Lead to Trauma and Disrupt Relationships." (April 11, 2008) http://www.ncptsd.org/facts/veterans/fs help for vets html.

Schiraldi, G. R. *The Post-Traumatic Stress Disorder Sourcebook: A Guide to Healing, Recovery, and Growth.* Los Angeles: Lowell House, 2000.

Stars and Stripes Military Newspaper. (articles from 2000-2008) various authors,

 gathered worldwide, Subjects: *Combat stress and Trauma.*

Thomas, Lowell. *Doolittle, A Biography.* Garden City, NY: Doubleday, 1976.

Trudeau, G.B. *The War Within: One More Step at a Time.* Kansas City, MO: Andrews McMeel, 2006.

Turak, Megan. "Nation Should Be Grateful for Military Service People." *News and Leader*, November 11, 2007. Springfield, Missouri.

CPSIA information can be obtained at www.ICGtesting.com
Printed in the USA
LVOW10*0635241214

419507LV00002B/15/P